A Banker's Insights on International Trade

Tips, Techniques and Tales from Practical Experience

Roy Becker

FOREWORD

I am delighted that Roy Becker has finally put into print his several real world stories of what can happen in the often confusing world of international trade. Roy has been a guest lecturer on several occasions in my graduate course on exporting. Over his visits I have heard most of the stories in this book. The students love the stories as they always provide a real, and usually humorous, example that emphasizes the point being discussed.

Drawing on his many years of banking experience, many of the stories relate to methods of payment (e.g. letters of credit), a topic which students often find confusing. The stories clarify the concepts in a way that retains them in the student's memory bank far longer than does a dry academic discussion. Thus, I believe this book will provide a very valuable supplementary resource in courses discussing such topics. However, the book also includes insights on how one can develop a career in international business, and other interesting topics. The book is particularly useful because Roy has listed the major concepts in "Learning Objectives" at the beginning of each story. There is also a very good index at the end of the book that allows the reader to quickly locate appropriate stories for a particular topic.

The stories are all short, sweet, and to the point; they make their point quickly and clearly. Perhaps most important, one comes away after reading the stories with the clear message that a good sense of humor is an invaluable asset when conducting international trade. It also helps to be able to laugh at one's self. If you have ever sought the answers to such burning questions as:

Which is better, #2 yellow corn, or #3?
How do you avoid getting burned on a Canadian check?
What do chickens without legs, and cows that are 24 months pregnant,
have in common?
How swift is S.W.I.F.T.?

then this book is for you! If you think the answers to these questions aren't relevant to your business, you might want to take a look. This is a good read; I highly recommend it.

David Hopkins, Ph.D.
Director of International Business Programs
The Daniels College of Business
University of Denver

TESTIMONIALS

Frank Reynolds, author, "*Incoterms for Americans*":

"If ever a topic needed hands-on instruction coupled with lighthearted humor, it's international payment terms. Fortunately, banker-instructor Roy Becker, rides to the rescue with his "*A Banker's Insights on International Trade.*" Every one of its fifty-two stories contains an important lesson, couched in some very funny anecdotes. This book will literally have you laughing all the way to the bank."

Tamantha L. Peters, BA MSc
Adjunct Professor of Economics and Director, Educational Services
The Metropolitan State College of Denver and World Trade Center Denver:

Roy Becker's book, "*A Banker's Insights on International Trade,*" is an excellent and well-needed contribution to existing applied business reference materials. The illustrative stories, with their learning objectives, are an excellent practical complement to the theoretical, textbook-based information presented in classes and seminars. The stories provide ready-to-use case studies, making the instructor's job much easier. Students can't help but learn from the humorous and insightful examples of real-life business experiences. This book should be required reading for any class in international business.

A Banker's Insights on International Trade

Tips, Techniques and Tales from Practical Experience

By Roy Becker

Second Printing
Copyright©MMII

First Printing
Copyright©MM

All rights reserved.
No part of this book may be used or reproduced in any manner
whatsoever without the written permission of the author
and the publisher.

Printed in the United States of America.

Cover design by Heidi Domagala

ISBN 0-9679927-0-2

A Banker's Insights on International Trade

Tips, Techniques and Tales from Practical Experience

Published by

Roy Becker Seminars
PO Box 3042
Littleton, CO. 80161-3042

Order Information
To order more copies of this book,
please use the order form at the back of this book
or contact Roy Becker Seminars at the above address.

Acknowledgments

I have always enjoyed training one-on-one or groups. A few years ago, I became aware of the importance of using stories to illustrate points in my presentations. Then I received telephone calls from participants who would say to me: "You don't remember me, but I was in a class you taught several months ago. Our company is involved in a particular situation and we think you can help." When I would ask, "What caused you to call me?" they would often answer, "Our situation reminds us of one of the stories you told in class." No one has ever said, "It reminds us of point number three on your outline!"

Based on a tip I learned at a workshop at the Colorado Speakers Association a few years ago, I developed titles for my stories, numbered them and listed them on a sheet of paper with a caption that is now the title of this book. In my presentations I provided the titles to the audiences and referred to the list when I used one of the stories. In order to break the routine, I would occasionally allow a member of the audience to choose a story from the list. After the presentation, many would indicate they wished there had been more time for stories.

As the list of stories grew, I prepared a script of each story. After several people found out about my script and encouraged me to publish the stories, I decided to make the jump from speaker to author. I have learned that writing requires more precision than verbally telling stories. The written word may travel farther and come under closer scrutiny. As a result, I would like to state that the facts, figures, and names found in these stories are as accurate as I know them. If errors are discovered by the readers, I invite you to contact me so the record can be set straight.

These stories would not exist except for the work experiences I have been fortunate to have. I want to thank my employers, all of them banks in Minnesota and Colorado, for providing the work experiences. Thanks to the companies who have allowed me to serve them as a banker and who have in fact, provided most of the material for these stories.

Others too, deserve thanks. My Toastmasters club helped me to hone my presentation and story telling skills. Participants in the workshops and seminars allowed me to test and improve the content of the stories. Co-workers, especially those who have taught me to see the humor in work and life, have been an integral part in developing the stories. The Colorado Independent Publishers Association (CIPA) provided practical information on the production and marketing of this work.

Certain individuals deserve recognition as well. The first person who asked to read my script was Frank Reynolds, author of a successful book, *"Incoterms for Americans."* I have saved, and will always cherish, a voice mail he left for me: "I read your stories. I have only two words for you: Print it!" Thanks, Frank, for the encouragement.

Dr. Dave Hopkins, Director of International Business Programs, University of Denver, has heard most of these stories from my visits to his classes. After reading the draft of this book, he encouraged me when he said he would make the book required supplemental reading in his classes. I was not sure how to feel, however, when he said he enjoyed reading the stories more than listening to them! Thanks, too, Dave, for providing valuable editorial comments.

Nan Hinton, a peer, assisted by making suggestions to clarify some technical issues. Steve Deyo provided valuable technical and editorial suggestions. Heidi Domagala used her creativity to develop the cover design, and Eric Bosley of Cire Printing and Promotions, skillfully took all the intangibles and created the tangible product.

My daughter, Nicki Jo, assisted by putting her journalism training to good use. She was the proofreader who noticed, and insisted, that I correct the curls on the quotation marks that were facing the wrong way. Nicki Jo also made many other valuable editorial comments and suggestions.

Roy Becker

Dedication

This book is dedicated to my wife Jean, and my children, Sonya and her husband Jeff, Mike and his wife Mary, and Nicki Jo. Their support, encouragement, and assistance served as daily inspiration to bring this book to life. Jean and Nicki Jo allowed me nights away to teach classes which ultimately resulted in the birth of these written stories. They also tolerated the evenings at the computer developing the manuscript.

CONTENTS

		Page
Foreword		v
Acknowledgements		xi
Introduction		xvii

Story #	**Title**	
1	The Nigerian Cement Story	1
2	Which Is Better, #2 Yellow Corn, or #3?	3
3	The Kind of Letter of Credit You Don't Want	5
4	How a Sneeze Led to a Career in International Banking	7
5	Training During The West Coast Dock Strike	9
6	Who Writes the Letter of Credit Rules?	11
7	How to Avoid the Most Common Error of Letters of Credit	13
8	The Infamous Monday in Brazil	15
9	Two Tips to Avoid Getting Burned On a Canadian Check (or When Cash In Advance Isn't)	17
10	The Confirmed Letter of Credit from the Philippines	19
11	The Unconfirmed Letter of Credit	21
12	How Do They Say "Hello" in France at 4 a.m.?	23
13	Where Does Risk Pass?	25
14	When a Mouse is an Elephant	27
15	Seven Factors for Determining the Right Method of Payment	29
16	You Can Export the Whole Pig -- Except the Squeal!	31
17	The Legal Aspects of a Bill of Lading	33
18	What do Chickens without Legs and Cows that are 24 Months Pregnant Have in Common?	35
19	What Are the Two Most Important Articles of the UCP?	37
20	July 12th: The Day Imports Equaled Exports	39
21	Investing at 50 Percent in Mexico	41
22	How Swift Is S.W.I.F.T.?	43
23	A Former School Teacher Exporting From a Storage Shed	45
24	The Hidden Expiration Date on Every Letter of Credit	47
25	If You Must Use Letters of Credit -- Get Them Right!	49
26	Back to Back Letters of Credit	51
27	Was the Whole Family Stow-aways?	53
28	When a Confirmed Letter of Credit Isn't	55
29	Mismatched Gardening Gloves	57
30	How I Learned Never to Make Sales Calls With Chinese Food on my Tie!	59
31	Khaki Pants that Will Keep You in Stitches	61
32	How I Won a Telemarketing Award	63
33	A Letter of Credit Used in an Organ Transplant	65

Story #	Title	Page
34	What is an Engineer's Certificate?	67
35	The Only Thing Hotter than a Hot Potato Is a . . .	69
36	They Thought They Were Importing Cue Sticks, What They Got Was . . .	71
37	How a Transposition Cost $300,000.00	73
38	Why Josie Heath Lost an Election	75
39	The American Flag, Mother, Apple Pie, and . . . Ex Works?	77
40	How an Oil Company Recovered Their Losses	81
41	How Germinating Seeds Brought Ten Cents on the Dollar	83
42	Eight Tips on How to Get Paid With a Letter of Credit	85
43	Who Saw the Goods?	87
44	Who is at Fault?	89
45	Acme's Freight Forwarding Company	91
46	How to Create an Earthquake	93
47	Eighteen Neophyte Exporters	95
48	Swimming Across the Pacific	97
49	The Great Salad Oil Swindle	99
50	The Golden Rule	101
51	Why Doesn't Everyone Use DDP?	103
52	The British Need Cement	105

Appendix
- Publications Information — 107
- Sample Letter of Credit: S.W.I.F.T. Format — 108
- Instructions to the Buyer for Issuing a Letter of Credit — 109
- Transaction Flow-charts — 111

Index of Key Terms — 113
Order Form — 117
About the Author — 120
Uniform Customs and Practice for Documentary Credits (UCP 500) — Insert

Introduction

Most of these stories provide information revolving around the terms of payment used in international trade. A brief overview of those terms may assist readers in better understanding the stories.

Four payments terms are commonly used for international trade: **cash in advance**, **open account**, **documentary collections**, and **letters of credit**.

Cash in advance is relatively easy to understand. The seller simply says, "Send me the money and I'll ship the goods." If the buyer agrees, the buyer has to trust the seller to ship the goods which conform to the purchase order. The buyer takes all the risk and the seller takes no risk.

On the opposite end of the risk scale, **open account** allows the buyer to receive and inspect the goods before they have to pay for them. If the buyer can negotiate extended terms, they may even be able to sell the goods to another buyer(s) and collect payment before they have to pay the supplier. The seller, on the other hand, trusts the buyer completely to pay as agreed. Here, the seller takes all the risk and buyer takes no risk.

In the above two methods of payment, only one party takes risk. The buyer takes the risk on **cash in advance** and the seller takes the risk on **open account**. The money side of international trade is relatively easy to understand when only one party takes the risk. Sometimes, neither party is willing to bear all the risk, so these two methods of payment will not accommodate the transaction, and the two parties must compromise and share the risk. The next two methods of payment are compromise payments. Each party must be willing to bear some risk.

A **documentary collection** method of payment provides a measure of protection for each party. The seller's risk is partially protected because the buyer cannot get the goods until they pay for them. After shipment, the seller submits the shipping documents to their bank on a collection basis. The documents are sent to the buyer's bank with instructions that the documents are to be released to the buyer only after payment is collected. The buyer cannot get the goods without the documents. If the buyer's bank is unable to collect payment, the seller considers the best of four options: 1) return the goods, 2) find another buyer, 3) renegotiate the payment with buyer, or 4) abandon the goods. The buyer, on the other hand, has proof of shipment, but has risk associated with paying on receipt of documents only. They hope the goods will conform to those described in the documents. If desired, the buyer may require the goods be inspected at the point of shipment to mitigate the risk of unacceptable goods. As demonstrated, each party has to bear some risk, and also has means to mitigate the risk. A flowchart of a collection transaction can be found in the Appendix on page 111.

When the parties agree to a **letter of credit**, the seller informs the buyer that the shipment will be made upon receipt of an acceptable **letter of credit**. The buyer instructs their bank to issue the **letter of credit** in favor of the seller. The bank makes a commitment to pay the exporter upon presentation of certain specified documents. Usually, some form of shipping document is required as proof that the seller has turned the goods over to a transportation company. Upon receipt of the **letter of credit**, the seller ships the goods, assembles the required documents and presents them to the bank for payment. The bank determines that the documents conform to the terms of the **letter of credit**, remits payment to the exporter and releases the documents to the importer. As mentioned, each party compromises in the sharing of risks. The exporter does not have to worry about the buyer's ability to pay and is willing to believe that the issuing bank will honor their letter of credit. The importer is willing to believe that the goods will conform to the documents presented for payment against the **letter of credit**. A flowchart of a **letter of credit** transaction can be found in the Appendix on page 112.

Uniform rules have been developed to provide worldwide standardization for many international transactions. Since no two transactions are alike, each payment for goods has its own unique story to tell. As in most human endeavors, communication is key for successful international sales transactions. Insufficient information, language barriers, and different expectations can cause misunderstandings. Everyone must be on his toes – including the banker.

The stories that are in this book are the result of situations in which importers, exporters, bankers, and transportation companies have found themselves. For the most part, the banker is the author. In some cases, the stories are from other sources and are easily identified. It is my hope that the stories will be educational, entertaining and inspiring.

Roy Becker

Story #1

The Nigerian Cement Story

Learning Objective:
- a) Understand the subtleties of sovereign risk
- b) Understand the protection of a confirmed letter of credit
- c) Key Terms: Letters of Credit, Risk, Confirmed Letter of Credit, Confirming Bank, Issuing Bank, Sovereign Risk

When Nigeria struck oil in the mid 70's, it became a cash-rich country. As a result, the Nigerians began to import large quantities of consumer goods. The goods arrived at a much faster pace than the out-of-date ports could handle. Ships were sprouting up in the harbor like weeds in an untended garden. Because the ports were so out-dated, they could bring only one ship in to dock at a time, unload it, send it back out and bring in the next ship. Crowded conditions slowed unloading by as much as six months. (I have heard some claims that it was as long as 24 months, which I have not been able to verify.) Ship owners were paying up to $4,000 a day in demurrage charges (a charge for the detention of a ship beyond the time allowed for unloading).

The government conducted a survey of the situation and determined they would need five million metric tons of cement to upgrade the port facilities. The problem was compounded when five ministers in the government thought it was their responsibility to order the cement. Consequently, orders were placed for 22 million tons of cement. When over 250 cement ships arrived, they only further added to the congestion and, of course, they were unable to unload. After about six months of waiting on the high seas, in the hot and humid weather, you can probably guess what happened to the cement! It took on moisture, hardened, and became useless while it was still on board the ships.

The government immediately went to the banks and said, "If you issued letters of credit for shipments of cement, don't pay." What would the banks do? They obeyed the law of the land and they didn't pay. If a shipper of cement had an irrevocable letter of credit from a Nigerian bank, suddenly it became a useless piece of paper.

How does one foresee a risk such as this? The answer is: you don't. You could have the best international economist on staff who monitors and plots every possible economic trend they can find. However, there are no statistics for "stupid mistakes" which is what we have in this story. Five ministers making a stupid decision. Since economists don't track stupid mistakes, they can't possibly predict: "Well, I think the trend shows we are due for a stupid mistake!"

How can an exporter be protected in a scenario such as this? By having the letter of credit "confirmed" by another bank in another country. When a bank confirms another bank's letter of credit the confirming bank is in essence guaranteeing payment. It is just the same as if the confirming bank issued the letter of credit themselves and they are obligating themselves to pay even if they cannot collect from the issuing bank for any reason. In this story, some confirming banks found themselves in the position of having to pay the exporters, but unable to collect from the Nigerian banks. It's the protection, or insurance, that an exporter wants, and the risk a bank has to be willing to take if it confirms another bank's letter of credit.

This story is an excellent example of sovereign risk. Sovereign risk can concisely be defined by asking the question: "Can the government intervene in any way to prevent payment from being made?" Sovereign risk includes the stability of the government and the economy.

This story also introduces the technique of a confirmed letter of credit. Story numbers 8, 9, 21, and 28 illustrate other examples of sovereign risk and story numbers 10, 11, and 28 provide instructions on how to get a letter of credit confirmed so it meets your standards of acceptability.

Now, the end of the story: What happened to the ships? The story circulated is that the cost of trying to chip the cement out of the holds was greater than the cost of the ships, so they sank the ships and, if so, I assume they are still there on the bottom of the ocean, off the coast of Nigeria.

Note: I first heard this story when I attended a seminar conducted by Jim Harrington, of (formerly) Bankers Trust in New York, in the late 1970s. Since then I have verified what I could and have slightly revised and embellished the story based on others' recollections of this incident.

Story #2

Which Is Better, #2 Yellow Corn, or #3?

Learning Objective:
    a)   Understand that one of the cornerstones of a letter of credit is "strict compliance"
    b)   Learn about the UCP
    c)   Key Terms: Uniform Customs and Practice (UCP), Commercial Invoice, Letter of Credit, Merchandise Description, Strict Compliance, Documents, Sales Contract

The Uniform Custom and Practice for Documentary Credits ("UCP") article 37c states: "The description of the goods in the commercial invoice must correspond with the description in the credit." What does this mean to an exporter? What does it mean to a bank? Every letter of credit will indicate a description of the merchandise which is to be shipped. To the bank, it means the merchandise description on the invoice must be exact, ver batim, identical to that on the letter of credit. Punctuation must be identical. Capital letters, and spaces must be identical. Why? Read on.

I conducted a workshop on letters of credit for a staff of commodity traders. They told me they were frustrated by their bank's interpretation of a letter of credit. The letter of credit described the merchandise as "#2 Yellow Corn or Better." The company shipped #1 Yellow Corn and described it on the invoice as "#1 Yellow Corn." They were astonished as they said to me, "The bank rejected the invoice! Why would they do that?" I answered, "I would have done the same thing! Remember, we are just bankers. We cannot be experts in all kinds of merchandise we see in the documents which come across our desks. I'm sure in the first ten minutes on the job as a commodity trader, you learned the grading system for corn. However, I am not a commodity trader. How do I know #1 is better than #2? Maybe #3 is better than #2. Since I can't possibly know everything about every type of merchandise, my role can be nothing more than to precisely compare the merchandise description on the invoice to that of the letter of credit." As one insightful attorney advised me early in my career, "Roy, your job is to compare, not interpret." Good advice.

I suggested a possible alternative to the traders. Since the invoice must precisely describe the merchandise as shown on the letter of credit, I suggested they prepare an invoice which describes the merchandise with a caption identical to the letter of credit, "#2 Yellow Corn or Better." Then, below the caption the invoice may carry a notation that the merchandise actually shipped was "#1 Yellow Corn." I believe a bank would find this acceptable.

Regardless of what was actually shipped, it is important that the merchandise description shown on the invoice precisely match the description stated in the letter of credit in order for the exporter to receive payment. This is the cornerstone of "strict compliance." Article 4 of the UCP goes on to state, "In Credit operations all parties concerned deal with documents, and not with goods." In other words, a bank does not care what was shipped, or even if anything was shipped at all. An exporter must simply supply documents that strictly comply with the terms of the letter of credit to be entitled to payment from the bank's letter of credit. The underlying sales contract and the shipment itself are not of concern to the bank.

Other "strict compliance" related stories are: numbers 18, 27, and 35.
"Autonomy" related stories include: numbers 36, 37, and 40.
Stories related to the prevention of discrepancies are: 7 and 25.
Stories that are related to the UCP include: 3, 5, 6, 11, 19, 24, 37, and 40.

Story #3

The Kind of Letter of Credit You Don't Want

Learning Objective:
- a) Learn the two major types of letters of credit
- b) Become acquainted with the purpose of the "UCP"
- c) Key Terms: UCP, Revocable, Irrevocable, Beneficiary

The wording of the Uniform Customs and Practice for Letters of Credit ("UCP") states in Article 6a: "A credit may be either revocable or irrevocable." (Please read story number 6 for a fuller explanation of the history and purpose of the UCP). Article 6 continues: "The Credit, therefore, should clearly indicate whether it is revocable or irrevocable. In the absence of such indication, the Credit shall be deemed to be irrevocable." Exporters may get lulled into thinking all letters of credit are irrevocable. However, very recently, a bank I worked for received a letter of credit clearly marked "revocable" from a bank in a Central European country for an exporter in Colorado Springs. We called the exporter to alert them and, not surprisingly, it was not what they were expecting, and they rejected the letter of credit.

What is the difference between a revocable and irrevocable letter of credit? According to UCP article 8: "A revocable Credit may be amended or canceled by the Issuing Bank at any moment and without prior notice to the beneficiary." So a good question to ask is, "Who would accept one?" The answer is: "No one." I have seen a revocable credit only in a rare situation such as a company using a revocable letter of credit to make purchases from an agent in Asia who was actually on the company's payroll. Since there was a high trust factor between the parties, it worked well. The agent knew the letter of credit would not be canceled, or if so, they would receive ample notice from the company. By using a revocable credit, the company saved themselves considerable bank fees. While it worked well to meet their needs, it was not a normal situation.

Because letter of fees vary widely among banks, and can be rather complicated depending on the transaction, I will deliberately avoid giving examples of fees of letters of credit. Nevertheless, fees for a revocable letter of credit would likely be priced less than half of an irrevocable letter of credit. As indicated, a bank has little risk because the bank can cancel the revocable letter of credit anytime and their fees will reflect this. Bank fees should be known well in advance of the transaction to avoid surprises. Banks are willing to discuss fees on a case by case basis with importers and exporters.

UCP article 9.d.i., on the other hand, states that an irrevocable letter of credit cannot be canceled or changed without the agreement of the beneficiary. If you are the beneficiary, it is the kind you do want. All you need to know about a revocable letter of credit is: it's the kind you don't want! Many stories in this series refer to other articles of the UCP.

> **"There is no typical pathway to any career."**
>
> See Story #4

Story #4

How a Sneeze Led to a Career in International Banking

Learning Objective:
    a)   How Careers Happen

University students who aspire to a career in international business often ask me, "How did you get into international banking?" My story, I assume, is as different as any one else's. As I look back at important happenings in my life, often I can see three turning points that occurred to obtain the final results. Those turning points were usually not of my doing, but the result of circumstances, fate, or whatever you want to call it. I'd like to think it is divine intervention. This is true of my career path as well. Who would have ever thought a shy, naive teenager who grew up on a farm in the upper Midwest would ever have a career in international banking?

The first turning point is very clear in my memory. As a teenager, I was expected to work on the family farm as a duty. I received no pay for working on the family farm, and none was expected. If I wanted some spending money, however, I would work for other farmers who needed help, usually during the harvest seasons. When harvesting a crop, a billowing cloud of crop dust would continually surround us. Unfortunately, I was allergic to the dust. I would sneeze, wheeze, and cough all day, then go home and try to sleep. Sleep didn't come easily since I would continue the sneezing, wheezing, and coughing through the night. But if I wanted the spending money, I had to get up the next morning and do it all over again. I remember one hot summer day I was on a flatbed helping a farmer put up his hay. The misery of the heat, the dust, and the humidity all got to me. I looked to the western horizon longing to see a single cloud which may eventually drift our way to provide some shade and relief from the sun and heat. I even dared to hope the cloud might have some rain which would cause us to quit work early that day. However, no cloud was visible. It was at that moment that I resolved: some day I would have a job in an air-conditioned office. That was turning point number one and it was a firm and clear resolve.

Turning point number two was an event that took me to the big city of Minneapolis and eventually into a banking career. As a teen, my hobby was tinkering with radios and TVs trying to figure out why they worked and trying to fix them if they didn't. I thought it might be a career of interest to me. So, I took my new bride and we moved to Minneapolis and I enrolled in a trade school to learn electronics. Due to several reasons, it didn't work out as anticipated. In an effort to find work, I approached an employment agency that sent me on several interviews, including one at a bank. I decided to accept the job as a teller in the cash vault, "until something better came along." Nothing ever has and this first job started me on a life-long career path in banking.

One early position I held was in the bank's credit department. When I interviewed for that position my manager told me that after two years he and I would go to the human resources department to look for a job transfer. This seemed like a strange comment on the day I accepted the job, so I asked him to elaborate. He said the type of work I would be doing would grow boring after about two years, and if it didn't, I shouldn't be doing it in the first place. True to his word, after two years we went to Human Resources to inquire about open positions in the bank and turning point number three surfaced.

One of the positions available was in the international department. The head of the international department told me the position involved working with letters of credit. I asked, "What is a letter of credit"? He answered, "I'll show you." He took me to the eighth floor of the bank and we entered a room containing about 15 desks with no partitions. Phones were ringing constantly and people were yelling to each other across the room. He related, "This is it." I viewed the chaos and replied, "I still don't know what a letter of credit is and I don't think this looks like a very attractive place to work." We went back to Human Resources to look into the other openings. Three weeks later when no other jobs materialized, the international manager called me again and told me he would like me to reconsider. He told me all the positive reasons why the international department would be a good place to work and why he thought I was the right person for the job. After sufficient stroking of my ego, I accepted. I did wonder about his sincerity three weeks later when he resigned and left banking altogether. However, this turning point number three did get me into international banking and only after completing a frustrating training period (see story number 5) did I begin to realize that this was where I wanted to be to continue my banking career.

Perhaps there is no typical pathway to any career, and certainly not in international business. I relate this story to show what can happen when you "follow your nose."

Story #5

Training During The West Coast Dock Strike

Learning Objective:
   a)   Learn how a bank handles discrepant documents against letters of credit
   b)   Key Terms: Documents, Letters of Credit, Discrepancies, Customs, Approval, UCP

In story number 4 I related how I began working in a bank's international department. What I did not elaborate upon were the circumstances that surrounded my first few months on the job. One reason the department was hiring was because of a workload that was unmanageable as a result of a U.S. West Coast dock strike that had just ended. All the pent-up shipments were now being released. Consequently, the daily deliveries of mail and couriers brought packages upon packages containing shipping documents to be processed for payment against letters of credit.

Doug, the letter of credit supervisor, had hurriedly promoted secretaries to the positions of document examiners. He hired me, and 12 days later, before I was fully trained, he hired another employee and asked me to train the new employee. Doug himself was rarely available to handle problems and answer questions because he was on the telephone eight hours a day counseling customers whose lives were also complicated by the dock strike. This was the work environment into which I entered.

On my first day I was given a set of self-paced training manuals. After reading the books I felt I had a pretty good handle on the topic, from a textbook perspective, anyway. But I quickly learned how the textbook differs from the real world.

When I was ready for my first real transaction I was assigned to examine a set of documents against a letter of credit which our bank had issued. The transaction was an importation of giftware from Japan. I checked the documents and found about eight "discrepancies" in the documents. Since the textbooks hadn't covered anything like this, I wasn't sure what to do next. I waited until Doug was between phone calls and told him what I thought to be a rare occurrence – eight discrepancies! Since the importer was a high volume customer, Doug knew them well. He simply instructed me to call the treasurer of the importer and tell him what the discrepancies were. "He'll 'waive' the discrepancies," Doug said. So I called the treasurer and true to Doug's prediction, the treasurer said, "I don't care about the discrepancies, I just want the goods. Please make payment and send me the documents so I can clear the goods through customs." This is normal bank operating procedure – to obtain the importer's approval prior to making payment when the documents contain discrepancies.

If the importer wants the goods, they'll authorize the payment. While a bank does have the right to refuse payment without consulting the importer, a bank normally will call the importer first. It is not the bank's desire to stand in the way of international trade. If the buyer wants the goods, let the transaction proceed. A bank will only refuse payment if so instructed by the buyer, or if the bank is at risk because the buyer is insolvent or some such reason.

I went on to check my next set of documents and once again found a number of discrepancies which were also "waived" by the importer. I soon learned that I would probably find discrepancies in the majority of the documents I checked. If I didn't find discrepancies, I would check them again because I figured I must have missed something.

This story illustrates how a bank handles discrepancies. It is in accordance with the guidelines set forth in the UCP, article 14, which says a bank "may in its sole judgment approach the applicant for a waiver of the discrepancy(ies)." A bank does not want to stand in the way of trade but it is obligated to protect the buyer against risk. If the buyer is OK with it, so is the bank, in most cases.

Other stories which discuss discrepancies and refusal of payment are numbers 14, 31, 35, and 36.

Story #6

Who Writes the Letter of Credit Rules?

Learning Objective:
    a)   Learn the history and purpose of the UCP
    b)   Key Terms: Letters of Credit, International Chamber of Commerce, UCP

In the early 1900s as the large New York banks became more involved in financing international trade and issuing letters of credit, they discussed the need for a standardization of the way banks process and interpret letters of credit. A committee was formed to develop common rules and the banks agreed to these rules around 1915. I have seen a copy of these early rules and they would still be quite pertinent and valid today. Soon thereafter, banks in Europe saw the need to have rules as well. As time passed, it became apparent that banks all over the world should process and interpret letters of credit uniformly.

Again a committee was formed, with representation from many countries, under the auspices of the International Chamber of Commerce. The first universally accepted rules were published in 1935, entitled, "Uniform Customs and Practice for Documentary Credits," usually referred to simply as the "UCP." Since 1935 it has gone through several revisions, usually revised about every 10 or 12 years. Currently in force is the 1993 revision, International Chamber of Commerce Brochure No. 500. It is well written, in plain English (no legalese), and it is a must for anyone who works with letters of credit. Any interpretation of a letter of credit needs to be made in light of the articles of the UCP. Although you would not read the UCP for leisure reading, it is a document with valuable information. If you work with letters of credit you should have one close at hand. A copy of the UCP can be found inside the back cover of this book. You may also contact your local bank and request a copy.

While it may be true that it is the banks that spearhead the drive for each revision, many different interest groups are consulted and have a hand in its writing. These include shipping companies, insurance companies, exporters, and importers. It is a guide for anyone who works with letters of credit.

The UCP contains 49 articles. In story number 19, you will learn which two articles I feel are the most important.

> "Is there anything wrong
> with the exporter
> instructing the buyer
> what the exporter wants
> in a letter of credit?"
>
> See Story #7

Story #7

How to Avoid the Most Common Error of Letters of Credit

Learning Objective:
- a) Realize an exporter can, and should, be proactive in setting letter of credit payment terms
- b) Key Terms: Letters of Credit, Application for Letter of Credit, Amendment, Discrepancies

Many an exporter becomes frustrated when they have shipped the goods and then have to prepare documents to conform to the terms of the letter of credit. They suddenly realize they have to prepare or find certain documents which they did not anticipate; or they are unable to meet other surprise requirements. One frustrated exporter exclaimed to me, "Why would a foreign bank write a letter of credit with all these unacceptable terms and conditions?" That is a good question to ask! Let's discuss and find the answer.

Does a bank arbitrarily draw up the terms of a letter of credit? No! Then who tells them what to write into the letter of credit? The buyer, of course. Where does the buyer get the information? May I be so bold to suggest: the exporter? Since the buyer is the exporter's customer, is there anything wrong with the exporter instructing the buyer what the exporter wants in the letter of credit? As story number 29 illustrates, a buyer may be very grateful to receive instructions from the seller about the preferred terms.

One effective tip is to develop a template of instructions to the buyer for opening a letter of credit. Many banks already have a model which can be used as a guide. I suggest a separate template for each buyer. A sample "Instructions to the Buyer for Issuing a Letter of Credit" is found in the Appendix section on page 109. Later, making changes will be easy for each transaction and important details will not be forgotten. At a minimum, a list of "bullet point" items is a must, which includes important things such as the amount, shipping and expiration dates, required documents, merchandise description, irrevocability, etc. One exporter has developed a pro-forma letter of credit which is available next to their fax machine. When they receive an order, they acknowledge the order by fax. They also send a copy of the proforma letter of credit and state that their payment terms are a letter of credit, which is identical to the pro-forma, or alternatively, "we do take cash." They export $35 million annually to Europe alone with this technique. This is proof it can be done.

The second effective tip is so simple and effective. I first heard it from an exporter in Boulder and immediately thought, "Why didn't I think of that?" The exporter first uses technique number one, an instruction sheet, described above. Based on the instructions sent by the exporter, the buyer will complete an application for a letter of credit – a form provided to them by their bank that would issue the letter of credit. With the completed application form, the buyer is dictating to the bank the terms of the letter of credit as discussed in the second paragraph above. The exporter in Boulder instructs each buyer to fax a copy of the completed application form to them before the buyer takes it to the bank. This allows the exporter to review the terms and provide feedback and suggestions if it is not satisfactory. The intent is to resolve differences at this stage in the process rather than waiting for the letter of credit to arrive and then go through a long and expensive amendment process.

The title of this story may have been misleading, and it was intended to be so. Many people might think the most common error has to do with "discrepancies" in the documents as discussed in stories 5, 14, 31, 35, and 36. However, I feel the most common error is failing to be **proactive** early in the process. Being proactive will reduce or eliminate the discrepancies which crop up during payment time. Similar to the computer adage, GIGO (garbage-in-garbage-out), good instructions sent to the buyer will result in a well-written letter of credit, which will result in efficient collection of payment. Story number 25 also emphasizes the need to be proactive.

Story #8

The Infamous Monday in Brazil

Learning Objective:
- a) Understand sovereign risk
- b) Key Terms: Accepted Draft, Sovereign Risk, Letter of Credit, Documents Against Acceptance, DAA, D/A, Documentary Collection

An exporter in Metro-Denver sold goods to a distributor in Brazil (and many other countries). They had a long and satisfactory relationship with the distributor, and decided to offer terms of 180 days on an accepted draft basis. The documents were sent to a bank in Brazil with instructions to release the documents after the buyer "accepted" the 180 day draft and therefore was obligated to pay it at maturity. This method of payment is a documentary collection with a time draft, frequently referred to as "documents against acceptance"; sometimes it is abbreviated as DAA or D/A. Flowcharts of documentary collections are found in the Appendix section on page 111. For years this relationship worked well and the distributor always met their obligation.

In October of 1989, the exporter shipped goods valued at $76,000. The distributor in Brazil accepted the draft with the maturity date falling on a Monday in March of 1990. On the Friday before that Monday, the government of Brazil announced that at the end of business that day, the old Cruzado was no longer valid and a new Cruzeiro would be introduced on Monday. On Monday, the due date, the distributor authorized the bank to pay the $76,000. The bank informed them the transfer could not be made until a rate of exchange was set for the new currency and new regulations were implemented relative to wire transfers. Days and weeks elapsed before the new regulations were implemented. The distributor was then informed, according to the new regulations, they could only wire $1,200 a year out of the country. It doesn't take a calculator to figure out collection of the $76,000 receivable was going to take some time!

This is another illustration of sovereign risk as defined in story number 1. The government intervened to prevent payment from being made. The distributor was willing to pay and had the capacity to pay, but due to government control, could not pay. Other examples that address sovereign risk are story numbers 1, 21, 28, and 40.

The exporter in Colorado informed the distributor that until the $76,000 was settled, there would be no more shipments. The distributor in Brazil, however, depended on receiving these goods for his livelihood. In order to keep his reputation clean, he arranged for the payment to be made from an account that he happened to have in a bank in Miami. Subsequently, all shipments were made only on letter of credit terms.

"It is easy for a U.S. company to assume
that trade with Canada is 'pretend exporting'
because of the close proximity.
However, it indeed is a foreign country
with a different currency, different laws, different customs
and different banking practices."

See Story #9

Story #9

Two Tips to Avoid Getting Burned On a Canadian Check
(or When Cash In Advance Isn't)

Learning Objective:
    a)   Understand the subtleties of sovereign risk
    b)   Understand banking practices in Canada (and other countries) are not the same as in the U.S.
    c)   Key Terms: NSF, Wire Transfer, Collections, Final Clearance, Federal Reserve System, Sovereign Risk

A distributor in the west metro-Denver area received an order from a company in Canada for computer equipment. Taking proper precautions with a new customer, the distributor asked for payment before they would ship the goods. They received a check payable in U.S. dollars drawn on one of the major banks in Canada. They deposited the check in their bank who gave them immediate credit. (As with any check, the credit was given subject to final clearance). Just to be safe, the distributor waited a week in case the check might be returned. After a week with no returned check, they shipped the goods. Three weeks later the check was returned marked, "Non-Sufficient Funds." They were never able to collect the money or get the goods back.

It is easy for a U.S. company to assume that trade with Canada is "pretend exporting" because of the close proximity. However, Canada is indeed a foreign country with a different currency, different laws, different customs and different banking practices.

United States banking practices require banks to pay or return checks within 24 hours. If a bank does not return a check within 24 hours it is considered paid. Therefore, "Non-Sufficient Funds" checks are returned to the depositor within a few days from anywhere in the country.

Canada, however, may have different banking practices (Canada is used for illustration only, any country could have been named). The distance that the check must travel also affects the clearing time. A check indeed can be returned days, weeks, and even months after it is presented, which is what happened to our distributor friend.

The title to this story says I will give two tips. In fact, to get more than your money's worth, I am going to give three tips:

    First, ask the buyer in the foreign country to send a wire transfer instead of a check. Wire transfers are always good funds and are immediately available.

    Second, if you receive a check, especially if it is large, drawn on a foreign bank, ask your bank to submit it on a "collection basis" rather than for immediate credit. When the foreign bank honors the check and the funds have been deposited in your account, they are good funds and no longer subject to final clearance. You will want to hold your shipment until you receive notice that good funds are in your account.

Third, instruct your buyer to send a check in U.S. dollars drawn on a U.S. bank. It's easy for them to ask their bank to do this. You will receive an official bank check drawn on a U.S. bank which can be cleared through the Federal Reserve System for immediate collection. Since it is a bank check (as opposed to a customer's check) you can have confidence that the check should be honored.

This story illustrates that while doing business in Canada is relatively easy, one should bear in mind that there are unique differences in the Canadian banking system as compared to the United States. Stories 1, 8, 15, 21, and 28 illustrate other examples of sovereign risk.

Story #10

The Confirmed Letter of Credit from the Philippines

Learning Objective:
- a) Understand the importance of being proactive
- b) Understand a right way and a wrong way of asking for a confirmed letter of credit
- c) Key Terms: Confirmed Letter of Credit, Issuing Bank, Sovereign Risk, Sight, Tenor, Expiration Date, Advising Bank

Exporters generally understand the protection they receive with a confirmed letter of credit. They usually know the confirming bank is obligated to pay even if unable to collect from the issuing bank. However, some exporters do not fully understand how to effectively ask for a confirmed letter of credit. I would like to emphasize one very important principle in this story and then give a right way and a wrong way to ask for a confirmed letter of credit.

The most important point an exporter needs to understand when dealing with letters of credit of any kind, is the need to be **proactive**. This is stressed in a number of the stories in this series. This holds true for needing a confirmed letter of credit, as well. A second bank will consider confirmation of a foreign bank's letter of credit only if asked by the foreign bank. A bank will not confirm a letter based only on the request of the exporter. In order for the confirming bank to have any recourse to the issuing bank, the issuing bank must request confirmation from the confirming bank. It follows that a foreign bank will only request the confirmation if asked to by their customer, the buyer. It further follows that the buyer has no motive to ask the issuing bank to request the confirmation unless the seller insists that the buyer do so. Hence the need to be proactive. All that remains to be decided is who pays the fees. Either party can offer to do so.

Now, let's consider the right way and the wrong way to ask for a confirmation. The wrong way is to instruct the buyer to send a "confirmed letter of credit." An exporter did just that recently. They received a hard copy of a letter of credit issued by a bank in the Philippines. The letter of credit was very properly entitled, "Confirmed Letter of Credit." There was no indication from the advising bank that they had confirmed the letter of credit. Indeed, they had not been asked to add their confirmation. What did the exporter really have? Can a bank confirm its own letter of credit? No! For an exporter to be protected with a confirmed letter of credit it must be confirmed by a second bank in a second country. It serves no purpose for a bank to confirm its own credit. It does not protect the exporter against the risk of default due to sovereign risk or the risk of the issuing bank not having the resources to pay. It must be confirmed by a second bank in a second country to be of any value.

Therefore, the right way to ask for a letter of credit is to use the words as follows: "The letter of credit is to be confirmed by _____." You fill in the blank. Or you may say you want the letter of credit confirmed "by a bank acceptable to us," or you may even insert the name of a bank. However, if you do use a bank's name, be sure to contact them first to find out if they are willing to confirm the credit. They will want to know five factors: 1) the country; 2) the name of the issuing bank; 3) the amount; 4) the tenor, i.e., sight, 30 days sight, etc. and 5) the expiration date. At that time the bank can also give you a quote for the price of confirming the letter of credit so you can build it into the price of your product.

Other stories in this series that discuss confirmation or the need to be proactive are story numbers 7, 10, 25, and 29.

Story #11

The Unconfirmed Letter of Credit

Learning Objective:
    a)   Understand the importance of a confirmed letter of credit
    b)   Understand UCP Article 9
    c)   Key Terms: Confirmed Letter of Credit, UCP, Issuing Bank, Irrevocable Letter of Credit, Amendment, Beneficiary, Advised Letter of Credit

A number of years ago I worked with a co-worker who grew up in Cuba. The fact that English was her second language, brought up an interesting nuance with regard to letters of credit. I remember on one occasion I referred to a letter of credit as "unconfirmed." She gently corrected me, "If a letter of credit is unconfirmed, that means it was first confirmed and then the bank removed its confirmation, making it unconfirmed. But," she went on, "a bank cannot undo its confirmation once it has confirmed a letter of credit."

Was she right? She was grammatically correct, of course, but it raises an interesting question. Can a bank add its confirmation to a letter of credit and then at a later date notify the beneficiary it no longer wanted to have its name, reputation, and obligation attached to the letter of credit? Where can we turn to find an answer for a question such as this? The UCP, of course!

Article 9 (UCP) addresses the liability of the issuing and confirming banks. Paragraph d.i. states: "an irrevocable Credit can neither be amended nor cancelled without the agreement of the Issuing Bank, the Confirming Bank, if any, and the Beneficiary."

This article states, then, that once a bank has confirmed a credit, the letter of credit cannot be amended or canceled without the beneficiary's agreement. Removing a confirmation would require an amendment, which requires the beneficiary's agreement. In summary, a bank can rescind its confirmation but only if the beneficiary agrees. So, in fact, it is possible, but highly improbable.

After that conversation, my co-worker and I agreed to refer to letters of credit as "confirmed" or "advised." An "advised" credit implies it was not confirmed.

Other stories which discuss UCP articles are numbers 3, 5, 6, 19, 24, 37, and 40.

> **"I am a firm believer of humor in the workplace."**
>
> See Story #12

Story #12

How Do They Say "Hello" in France at 4 a.m.?

Learning Objective:
    a)   Realize the importance of humor in the workplace
    b)   Key Terms: International Wire Transfer, Beneficiary, Intermediary Bank

Many customers use international wire transfers when making payments overseas. This includes businesses that have to pay invoices as well as individuals that send money to relatives. A common procedure is for the customer to call their bank with the pertinent information, such as: amount to be transferred, beneficiary's name, address, bank, and bank account number. The customer's bank is known as the remitting bank. It is the remitting bank's responsibility to determine how to "route" the money to the beneficiary's bank, and to notify the beneficiary's bank that the money has been sent.

On rare occasions, for a variety of reasons, the money doesn't arrive promptly at the beneficiary's bank. In such cases, the remitting bank will trace the wire to determine where the money is and what went wrong, so it can be corrected and the funds properly remitted to the beneficiary.

A bank for which I worked, had a customer who asked us to send a payment to a beneficiary in France. A young man, Eric, in our department took the call. He recorded the information, determined the routing and informed the customer that the beneficiary should have the money in two to three days.

A week later, the customer called Eric and informed him that the beneficiary in France claimed non-receipt. Eric offered to put a tracer on the wire and promised the customer it would be quickly resolved.

Another week elapsed and again the customer called, somewhat less understanding this time, and informed Eric that the money still was not in France. Eric came into my office and asked, "Roy, if I get up at 4:00 tomorrow morning and call the bank in France from my home, will the bank pay for my phone call?"

I smiled to myself as I replied, "Eric, if you are willing to get up at 4.00 a.m., yes, the bank will pay for your phone call!"

The next morning, at a staff meeting, he related what had happened. He had called the beneficiary's bank in France. The bank's operator answered, "Bon jour." Eric, who knew no French, tried to explain that he needed to speak to someone in the international department who could speak English. After several phone transfers, he reached someone who could help. They discussed the transaction and finally determined the problem was with another bank in France, an intermediary bank, who apparently had failed to relay the money. Eric asked the employee at the French bank if she had the telephone number of the intermediary bank. She said she did and she read it to him.

Eric then dialed the number of the intermediary bank. As it rang the first time or two he again anticipated to hear, "Bon jour," and he expected he would again have to try to get to an English speaking person. What he heard, when the phone was answered, was the voice of a very young female, with a distinct American accent, who said, "Hello?" Of course, Eric was caught off guard. Since he knew he had carefully dialed the number, including country code and city code, he jumped right into his reason for calling, "Hello, my name is Eric. I'm calling from a bank in Denver, Colorado, and I'm trying to trace a wire transfer which we sent to you two weeks ago," and he went into a lengthy explanation of the problem. As he paused, the voice on the other end said, "Excuse me, do you think you are speaking to a bank?" "Why, yes," Eric replied, "to whom am I speaking?" "I'm an American student going to school here in Paris," she explained, "I was just walking down the street and heard this pay phone ringing!"

I have often reflected on this incident and continue to marvel at the remarkable sense of humor that Eric had. Most employees would have come in that morning, grumbling about how early they had to get up, and then, of all things, they ended up calling a pay phone! However, no one saw the humor in the situation better than Eric did, and as he told us the story, he had the whole office laughing at his misfortune.

I believe that humor in the workplace allows us to be more relaxed and handle stress and frustration more effectively, as stories 30 and 32 also illustrate.

> # Story #13
>
> # Where Does Risk Pass?

Learning Objective:
    a)   Obtain an introduction to Incoterms 2000
    b)   Realize the misuse of the terms FOB and Ex Works
    c)   Key Terms: International Chamber of Commerce, Incoterms 1990, Incoterms 2000, Ex Works (EXW), Bill of Lading, Free Carrier (FCA), Free On Board (FOB)

Early in my career, I heard debates on the topic: where does risk pass? It seemed, among bankers anyway, this debate was reserved for lawyers to argue in court. Now, however, thanks to the undertaking of the International Chamber of Commerce ("ICC"), we have the answer to the question.

In the recently published ICC publication, Incoterms 2000, we have definitions for each of the thirteen trade terms. In a well thought out sequence, it lists each Incoterm and then stipulates ten responsibilities for the buyer and ten for the seller. It addresses who jumps through the hoops and hurdles. For example, who pays for loading the inland carrier, who pays the cost of shipping to the main carrier, who pays for loading the main carrier, who pays for the cost of shipping on the main carrier, who pays for the insurance, who pays for unloading the main carrier, the inland freight, import customs, etc.? Each Incoterm defines who must take on these responsibilities: the buyer or the seller.

When the predecessor publication, Incoterms 1990, was published, it was written by a committee of 20 people, 19 who were from Europe and one from Japan. A noticeable absence of American representation. The ICC undertook to revise Incoterms again in 2000, and this time one American, Frank Reynolds, was invited to the committee. Incoterms can best be understood if read with a European mind-set. Many of the European countries can export products with the goods never leaving the surface of the earth: by truck, rail, barge, etc. As a result some Incoterms may not be applicable to American exporters and importers.

It is important that the correct Incoterm be used to facilitate payment. Two of the most misused Incoterms are EXW and FOB. For example, I have seen letters of credit issued to beneficiaries in Colorado stating "Ex Works, the seller's warehouse." That's easy to understand and it appears to be no hassle for the exporter. It essentially means, "the goods are at my back door, come and get them." However, the letter of credit calls for an "on-board" ocean bill of lading issued from a West Coast port. How is the exporter going to obtain the bill of lading? What if the merchandise is destroyed en-route to the port and they can't get a bill of lading? They've fulfilled their obligation under the Ex Works agreement but they can't get paid. In story number 43 I related two incidents of other surprising risks with the Ex Works quote.

What about FOB? It's a term as easy for an American to understand as the American flag. However, the term FOB, as Americans understand it, does not have the same meaning to the rest of the world. Our own Uniform Commercial Code defines FOB essentially as FOB here, there, or anywhere. As defined in Incoterms, the FOB quote is reserved for ocean shipments only. It is very precise in its definition that risk passes as the goods pass over the rail of the ship. Notice the word "ship." When terms such as "FOB our plant" or "FOB Airport" are used, they are used incorrectly for international shipments and there is no authoritative document to turn to in case of a dispute.

So what is the solution to the dilemma of Ex Works and FOB? The key lies in asking for the correct transport document, or using an alternative Incoterm. In the case of Ex Works, since there is no shipping responsibility for the seller, the transport document used for payment on a letter of credit could be a receipt obtained from the first carrier to pick up the goods, such as a freight forwarder's receipt or a truck receipt. (This solution disregards the risk that the buyer may never send a truck to pick up the goods). In the case of FOB (other than ocean shipments), a better Incoterm to use is "FCA," or Free Carrier. FCA is a flexible term and can be used for any mode of transport. It is easy for Americans to understand because it is similar to the American's beloved term "FOB."

Since there is an Incoterm for any situation, it is important to use the right one to prevent misunderstanding. Frank Reynolds' book, *Incoterms for Americans* provides valuable insight to enable American companies to avoid misunderstanding and problems. Ordering information for *Incoterms 2000* and *Incoterms for Americans* can be found in the Appendix on page 107.

Story #14

When a Mouse is an Elephant

Learning Objective:
    a)   Realize One of the Cornerstones of a Letter of Credit is Strict Compliance
    b)   Key Words: Letter of Credit, Documents, UCP, Commercial Invoice, Applicant, Beneficiary, Discrepancy, Amendment, Strict Compliance

Many years ago, an international banking guru by the name of Frank Sauter, with a New York bank, (formerly) First National City Bank, wrote a series of articles entitled, "Random Notes on Commercial Credits" which I have been fortunate to collect. This story is adapted from one of his articles.

A company in the United States placed an order with a company from a country other than Scotland, and asked the buyer to open a letter of credit to pay for the purchase. The merchandise description in the letter of credit read simply, "Scotch Whiskey." When the documents arrived at the issuing bank, they discovered the merchandise on the invoice read, "Scotch-type Whiskey", not "Scotch Whiskey" as required by the letter of credit. Article 37c of the UCP states: "The description of the goods in the commercial invoice must correspond with the description in the Credit." Did it? Does "Scotch-type Whiskey" mean the same as "Scotch Whiskey"? A cautious banker would properly conclude, "Why should I make the decision? I'll call the applicant and let them decide."

The applicant, too, wondered, "What is Scotch-type Whiskey?" The bank and the applicant concluded the best alternative was to give the beneficiary an opportunity to submit a correct invoice to read, "Scotch Whiskey." However, the beneficiary refused to substitute the invoice. Now everyone was suspicious. If the beneficiary refused to replace the invoice, perhaps they shipped something other than "Scotch Whiskey." They may have shipped a whiskey that was like Scotch, but not Scotch. The applicant decided not to "waive" the discrepancy. Payment was refused and the shipment was returned, and no one, except the shipper, ever knew what was actually shipped.

Many an exporter is frustrated by a bank's "nit-picky" examination of documents. It is the bank's obligation to pay under the letter of credit only if the beneficiary presents documents which comply with the terms of the letter of credit. Without correct documents a bank can only pay if the applicant waives the discrepancies. All legitimate discrepancies carry equal weight. A small discrepancy may seem to be a mouse to the exporter but to the importer looking for a way to refuse the payment, the discrepancy may be an elephant.

An exporter must prepare documents which strictly meet the terms of the letter of credit in order to demand payment from the bank. If unable, an amendment should be requested before shipment is made. Other stories that relate to the cornerstone of strict compliance include numbers 2, 18, 27, 35, and 36.

> "A proactive exporter
> will probably use all four methods of payment
> depending on the circumstances
> of their international business."
>
> See Story #15

Story #15

Seven Factors for Determining the Right Method of Payment

Learning Objective:
    a)   Understand Payment Risks
    b)   Key Terms: Letters of Credit, Risks, Confirmed Letter of Credit

I am often asked, "What is the best method of payment for international shipments?" Many bankers answer, "letters of credit." I believe this is a self-serving answer. Of all the methods, letters of credit generate the most fee income for a bank. I hope I have never used such a pat answer. My answer to the question is, "The one that gets the deal done to the satisfaction of both parties, the buyer and the seller. There may not be a perfect method of payment for either one, so both have to agree on a payment with which they both can live."

What then are the choices? On the next page you will find two grids. One shows the four methods of payment with an explanation of the risks to the buyer and seller. The other grid has seven key questions to ask. Seven questions should be asked for each and every international sale. By answering these questions, it should become obvious which payment is right.

I worked with an exporter who told me their sale terms were confirmed letters of credit. Period. It didn't matter if the letters of credit were issued by major British, German or Japanese Banks, they needed to be confirmed. I believe it is wrong for a company to set a policy for international payments to be confirmed letters of credit. A proactive exporter will probably use all four methods of payment depending on the circumstances of their international business.

In using the seven factors, an exporter can select the right payment for each transaction.

TERMS OF TRADE

	TIME OF PAYMENT	GOODS AVAILABLE TO BUYER	RISK TO EXPORTER	RISK TO IMPORTER
CASH IN ADVANCE	Before shipment is made	After payment	None	Relies on exporter to ship goods as ordered
LETTER OF CREDIT	When shipment is made	After payment	Very little, or none, depending on terms	Assured shipment is made but relies on exporter to ship goods as ordered
COLLECTION	On presentation of draft to buyer	After payment	If draft is unpaid, must dispose of goods	Same as LC unless allowed to inspect goods
OPEN ACCOUNT	As agreed	Before payment	Relies on buyer to pay as agreed	None

SEVEN FACTORS TO CONSIDER BEFORE SETTING PAYMENT TERMS

	CASH	LETTER OF CREDIT	COLLECTION	OPEN ACCOUNT
1. Customer relationship	New	New	Established	Established
2. Nature of order	Custom	Custom	Normal	Normal
3. Political situation	Unstable	Unstable	Stable	Stable
4. Economic situation	Unstable	Unstable	Stable	Stable
5. Competitors offer terms	No	No	Yes	Yes
6. Risk of price changes	Yes	Yes	No	No
7. Need to control cash flow	Yes	Yes	No	No

Story #16

You Can Export the Whole Pig -- Except the Squeal!

Learning Objective:
- a) To broaden one's horizons as to the variety of goods can be marketed overseas
- b) Learn how an assignment of proceeds can finance a purchase
- c) Key Terms: Letter of Credit, Air Waybills, Assignment of Proceeds

One of my "hobbies" is to browse through files of "letter of credit" transactions and simply read the merchandise description as stated in the letter of credit. Its amazing what people have been able to sell, and to ship overseas. One of my favorites is a trading company who specializes in animals and animal by-products.

The company received a letter of credit for a shipment of 240 live Holstein cows to be shipped to Korea. The letter of credit required a veterinarian's certification that each animal was pregnant. (The buyer in Korea wanted the cows to bear calves shortly after arrival). The beneficiary presented the required 240 certificates, each signed by a veterinarian. Another requirement of the letter of credit was the presentation of air waybills as proof of shipment. The exporter chartered a 747 from Moses Field in Washington. He entertainingly explained how the airlines had to build partitions in the aircraft so the animals would not all fall to the back of the aircraft on take-off, or to the front on landing!

How did he pay for the purchase of 240 pregnant Holstein cows and pay for the freight to ship them? He had received a letter of credit from a bank in Korea, which stipulated he could get paid as soon as he shipped the cattle. However, he did have to convince the dozen or so farmers who were willing to sell him the cows that they would have to wait for payment until he received payment from the letter of credit. He also had to convince the airline they would have to wait for payment of the costs of the charter. He came to our bank and asked us to issue a document called an "Assignment of Proceeds." With this document the bank obligates itself to pay proceeds directly to other parties (it was tempting to say "utter" parties) when payment is received on a letter of credit. An exporter may request a bank to issue an assignment of proceeds without the buyer's knowledge or approval. Amazingly, the farmers and the airline all agreed to this arrangement and the shipment and the transaction proceeded without a hitch.

This same customer received a letter of credit for a shipment of 20 container loads of smelt to Japan. Knowing that Minnesotans find the best use for this small fish to be fertilizer for their gardens, I asked him who was buying the smelt and for what were they using them. He said he was selling them to an airline in Japan who was serving them on flights and advertising the food as a delicacy.

Another letter of credit he received was for a shipment of tripe (the lining of the first stomach of a cow). It was being sold to Japan for use in their soups.

Several years passed and I had little contact with him. I met him again at the airport in Sioux Falls, South Dakota, as I was boarding a flight destined for Dallas with stops in Sioux City and Omaha. We arranged to sit together and I asked him where he was headed. He replied he was going to Omaha to visit a slaughtering house. When I asked what he was exporting, he said he was stopping in Omaha to buy gallstones retrieved from cows. He was exporting them to Japan for use in medicines. When I asked what the price was for cow's gallstones, he said it was $300 an ounce, roughly the same price per ounce as the price of gold.

Someday, I will not be surprised when an exporter tells me they have found a market for the squeal of a pig!

Story #17

The Legal Aspects of a Bill of Lading

Learning Objective:
a) To learn the importance of a bill of lading
b) Key Terms: "On-board" Date, Bill of Lading, Title Document, Letter of Credit, Collection

The shipping date is an important point on the time line in an international transaction. The payment date is usually tied to the shipment date in some way. Even the financing is often tied to the date, as banks often refer to "pre-shipment" or "post-shipment" financing. How does one know on what date the goods were shipped? The bill of lading is the document that determines the shipment date. For letter of credit purposes, it is the "on-board" date that is the date of shipment. How important is the bill of lading?

The bill of lading is extremely important in international trade because of its legal aspects. Legally, the bill of lading accomplishes three purposes:

1) It is a title document which means it conveys ownership. It can be issued in negotiable form so that whoever holds the bill of lading has title to the goods. This can be an important feature where control of the title is critical until the buyer pays for the goods.

2) It is a receipt for the goods. The carrier is saying, "We have the goods." The fact that the goods are in the hands of a third independent party is often the security a buyer wants before remitting payment.

3) It is a contract for delivery. The carrier states it will move the goods from point A to point B as instructed by the exporter.

These three qualities make the bill of lading a valuable document. Since it is a title to the goods, it can be issued in negotiable form and can be bought and sold. This is an advantage for the buyer who may have pre-sold the goods. The bill of lading can be simply endorsed to the next buyer in line. In fact, it can be bought and sold any number of times. Finally, the last endorser on the document must take possession of the goods when they arrive.

These features of a bill of lading are important when control of the documents is important such as in a letter of credit or collection transaction.

> **"While reading the merchandise description,
> a sense of humor is of some value."**
>
> See Story #18

Story #18

What do Chickens without Legs
and
Cows that are 24 Months Pregnant Have in Common?

Learning Objective:
- a) To learn the cornerstone of strict compliance
- c) Key Terms: Letter of Credit, Invoice, Strict Compliance, UCP

As I mentioned in story number 16, one of my work-related hobbies has been to review the files containing our export letters of credit. It is interesting to see the wide variety of goods which have been exported and paid by a letter of credit (see story number 16). While reading the merchandise description, a sense of humor is of some value.

We worked with an exporter who manufactured items a farmer uses when raising animals, such as steel fences with swinging gates, etc. They also manufactured "brooder stoves." When a farmer buys baby chicks, it is early spring and it is cold outdoors. Since the chicks are only one day old and are born with the instinct of crowding under the mother hen's wings to keep warm, they look for a place to keep warm. (She is commonly referred to as a "brooder" hen). The brooder stove is a substitute for the brooder hen. By means of electricity or natural gas, it gives off heat and the chicks crowd under it for warmth. As the weather gets nicer and the chicks grow bigger, the farmer raises the brooder stove off the floor by means of adjustable legs or with a rope hung from the ceiling's rafters, as my father did.

This manufacturer received a letter of credit in which the merchandise description was shown on the letter of credit as: "Brooder stoves for chickens without legs." While it is obvious what they really meant, the bank will look for an invoice which accurately and correctly describes the merchandise as: "Brooder stoves for chickens without legs."

What do the chicks have in common with cows that are 24 months pregnant? Only that they share the principle of strict compliance. Read on.

Remember our friend who could find a market for anything (story number 16)? I mentioned his sale of 240 live Holstein cows to Korea. Payment was on a letter of credit. After he had shipped the animals, he brought the documents in to the bank for examination and payment. One of my co-workers was assigned the task of the examination. After a short while she came to my desk and asked, "Roy, you grew up on a farm, didn't you? Can a cow be 24 months pregnant?" I replied, "No, the gestation period is nine months, just like a human." "Well," she said, "I have a letter of credit which says the cows are to be 24 months pregnant." I grabbed the file out of her hands and said, "Let me see that!" Sure enough, the merchandise description read, "Holstein cows 24 months pregnant." With a little thought, it became obvious that it should have read, "Holstein cows, 24 months old, pregnant." But in keeping with our cornerstone of strict compliance, we needed to see the invoice as, "Holstein cows 24 months pregnant."

While article 37c of the UCP states: "The description of the goods in the commercial invoice must correspond with the description in the Credit," it is more lenient with the merchandise description shown on the other documents: "In all other documents, the goods may be described in general terms not inconsistent with the description of the goods in the Credit."

Other stories which illustrate the cornerstone of strict compliance are numbers 2, 14, 27, 35 and 36.

Story #19

What Are the Two Most Important Articles of the UCP?

Learning Objective:
- a) To gain an understanding of the Uniform Customs and Practice for Documentary Credits
- b) Key Terms: UCP

The current revision of the Uniform Customs and Practice for Documentary Credits ("UCP") became effective on January 1, 1994. A copy has been inserted at the back of this book. For two years leading up to that date, the banking community was offered many seminars to become acquainted with the impact the changes would have.

The UCP has 49 articles covering items such as liabilities and responsibilities, what kind of signature is required on a bill of lading and a definition of the word "approximately." So which two articles are the most important?

I contend they are the silent articles, 50 and 51. Article 50 says, "The bank is always right." Article 51 says, "If the bank is ever wrong, refer to article 50!"

> **"Remember that an export to one country is an import to another."**
>
> See Story #20

Story #20

July 12th: The Day Imports Equaled Exports

Learning Objective:
- a) To think big
- b) Key Terms: Balance of Payments

It happened on July 12th of last year. Imports equaled exports. Exactly. I remember, because that is my birthday. However, it did not even make the Wall Street Journal, or the Financial Times. Why? Because it happens every day! If you simply remember that an export to one country is an import to another, then imports equal exports every day. In theory, of course. When the transactions actually get recorded, is another matter!

This may have been a bit of trickery on your mind. Most people would think of this topic in context of one country's balance of payments, which is defined as the record of transactions between one country and its trading partners in the rest of the world. In this context, imports would rarely if ever, equal exports. If viewed from a worldwide perspective, however, they are always equal.

> **"Any action on the part of the government can increase your risk."**
> **This is commonly referred to as sovereign risk.**
>
> See Story #21

Story #21

Investing at 50 Percent in Mexico

Learning Objective:
- a) To understand sovereign risk
- b) Key Terms: Sovereign Risk

I received a call from a customer who asked that we withdraw the money from his account and wire it to a bank in Mexico. This seemed a bit unusual so I asked him, "Is this for a gift to a relative, or are you purchasing some goods?" He replied, "No, it is for me." I asked if he was going to live in Mexico. He said, "No."

My curiosity and sense of duty caused me to inquire a little further. "Then why are you sending the money to Mexico?" I asked. "I have a friend working and living in Mexico," he said, "he told me that if I deposit the money in a Mexican Bank for one year, I will earn 50 percent interest."

I asked him if he considered the risks. "What risks?" he asked. "First," I said, "Is your deposit in pesos or dollars?" "It is in pesos," he replied. "Then you bear the risk of currency exchange rate differences and you could lose considerable money," I informed him, "furthermore, the government of Mexico could freeze your deposit and you may never get it back. Any action on the part of the government can increase your risk." This is commonly referred to as sovereign risk.

Then he inquired if he could transact a forward contract with the bank to protect himself against adverse rate movement. I asked him if he knew how forward rates are calculated to which he said, "No." I explained rates are very simply and precisely calculated using the interest rate differential between the two countries to determine the premium or discount on a forward rate. If he chose to leave the money in the U.S. and earn interest at prevailing rates, or chose to put pesos on deposit at a Mexican bank, earn interest, and lock in a forward rate, he will come out exactly the same at the end of the time period.

After considering the risks, and the possibility of no return at all, he decided to leave his money safely in the U.S. bank he trusted.

> **"S.W.I.F.T. now supports
> over 6,700 financial institutions
> in 189 countries."**
>
> See Story #22

Story #22

How Swift Is S.W.I.F.T.?

Learning Objective:
- a) To have an understanding of a basic international banking tool
- b) Key Term: S.W.I.F.T.

Technology continues to carry international banking to new heights. Two and three decades ago, messages were transmitted between banks via mail or telex. While quite adequate, both were somewhat slow, vulnerable to fraud, and lacked standardization. In the mid 1970s, with the advent of computers, a new communication tool was introduced to the international banking community. A cooperative was formed and took the name, "The Society for Worldwide Interbank Financial Telecommunication," or "S.W.I.F.T." It is similar to a private e-mail system for banks and other financial institutions who are members. S.W.I.F.T. continues to be on the cutting edge of technology. S.W.I.F.T. now supports over 6,700 financial institutions in 189 countries.

In order to enjoy the benefits, a bank must join the cooperative and buy only approved hardware and software. Every message type has a standard format. For example, Message Type 100 ("MT 100") is used only for wire transfers. The computer screen displays the format and data must be entered in each required field. When transmitted, the message received at the receiving bank will also be in the required format. As employees become familiar with the message types, they learn the messages are easy to input and to read, and as a result errors are reduced.

S.W.I.F.T. is also very secure. To the best of my knowledge, since its inception in the mid 70s there has yet to be a fraudulent message. The procedures that S.W.I.F.T. has implemented include the exchange of authenticator keys among member banks which must be changed periodically, upgraded equipment and software, and the encryption of messages. In December 1999, averages of 4.2 million messages a day were transmitted representing an estimated 5 trillion dollars daily.

As the acronym implies, it is also "swift." Messages are transmitted instantaneously through the system and received by the receiving party within a matter of seconds. More interesting facts and figures are available on their website, www.swift.com.

> **"One hundred percent of her sales were exports."**
>
> See Story #23

Story #23

A Former School Teacher Exporting From a Storage Shed

Learning Objective:
 a) To expand a person's thinking about export possibility

I have been fortunate to teach classes in Colorado at the World Trade Center Denver, the American Institute of Banking, as well as a guest lecturer at a number of area colleges and universities. While participants often provide positive feedback during or immediately after a session, few take time later to write a thank you note, and none is expected. Once, I did receive a very nice thank you note from a participant after teaching a class in the "Basics of Exporting Series" at the World Trade Center Denver. Since she was considerate enough to take time to write, I called her to thank her for the note. Our conversation led to a discussion of her business.

When I asked her about her interest in exporting, she invited me to come visit her at her place of business. After she gave me the address, we agreed on a day the following week. That day, as I was driving down the street looking for her address, I was in for surprise. The address she gave me coincided with a storage-shed facility. I drove past thinking I had written it down incorrectly. I found a telephone and called her to verify the address and she said, "Yes, my office is in one of the units in the storage facility." I drove back, turned into the address and found the unit with the door open. She was sitting at a desk with a cellular phone, surrounded by shelves containing boxes of small spare parts.

After a few pleasantries, I asked what her business was all about. She told me she buys antiquated broadcasting equipment which is no longer used in this country. She strips the equipment down for parts and sells the parts to other countries that still use the equipment in broadcasting. One hundred percent of her sales were exports.

She was a schoolteacher who took early retirement to pursue new challenges. You don't need a luxurious office, a storage shed will do just fine.

> **"One way the importer can force the exporter
> to deliver the documents to the bank
> is with a short presentation period requirement."**
>
> See Story #24

Story #24

The Hidden Expiration Date on Every Letter of Credit

Learning Objective:
- a) To become familiar with articles 42 and 43 of the UCP
- b) Key Terms: UCP, Expiration Date, Letter of Credit, Presentation Period, Customs Entry, Consular Invoice

The Uniform Customs and Practice for Documentary Credits ("UCP") states in article 42: "All Credits must stipulate an expiry date. . ." The expiry date can usually be easily found in the letter of credit. There is, however, another date that is just as important. It is referred to as the "date for presentation" in article 43. The presentation period is a window of time in which the exporter must present documents. It is usually tied to the date of the transport document.

The letter of credit will contain terminology similar to "documents must be presented within 10 days after the bill of lading date but within the validity of the letter of credit." For example, if the shipment took place on January 1st, documents must be presented no later than January 11th or the expiration date if earlier. If the expiration date is January 5th, documents must be presented by January 5th, not the 11th. Some letters of credit require a presentation period of seven days, some 15, etc. If the letter of credit is silent, the exporter has 21 days according to UCP article 43a. The exporter must be aware of this requirement and feel confident they can work with the stated time period. If not, an amendment should be requested. Why does a letter of credit have this requirement?

The importer stipulates this requirement because of a concern of their own. When the goods arrive at the customs entry point, the importer needs the documents to clear the goods. If not cleared in a timely manner the goods will go into storage and charges will be incurred, usually at monthly minimum rates. One way the importer can force the exporter to deliver the documents to the bank is with a short presentation period requirement. Once the documents are in the banking channels, they will find their way to the importer in due time for customs clearance.

An exporter, however, must be aware of several things. How quickly after shipment can they assemble the documents to get them to the bank? Are there any unusual situations that may cause delays? A common problem is the requirement of Consular Invoices. Can the exporter get a particular country's consular's signature within the time limit? Some consulates only sign documents once a week unless it is a holiday here or in their own country, then one must wait for another week. While 10, 15 or even 21 days may seem like adequate time, it can slip away quickly.

> "If there has been any message
> I have been preaching
> to customers
> the last few years,
> it is simply,
> 'Be proactive!'"
>
> See Story #25

Story #25

If You Must Use Letters of Credit -- Get Them Right!

Learning Objective:
- a) To learn how to be proactive
- b) Key Terms: Letter of Credit, Application for Letter of Credit

Too often an exporter receives a letter of credit and then is frustrated with the terms the issuing bank has provided. They ask, "Why would a bank issue a letter of credit with terms and conditions like this?" They do not understand that the issuing bank does not arbitrarily set the terms. If there has been any message I have been preaching to customers the last few years, it is simply, "Be proactive!"

Many exporters do not realize they can set the terms of the letter of credit. I suggest several possible ways to do this. First, provide a detailed proforma invoice that gives sufficient information to the buyer for opening a letter of credit. Second, provide detailed instructions to the buyer for opening the letter of credit. I have developed sample instructions that are included in the Appendix at the back of this book. Third, ask the buyer to fax a copy of the completed application for a letter of credit before they take it to their bank. This allows for feedback, revisions and agreement before the letter of credit is ever issued. The savings in time and money will be worth it.

Read story number 29 to have a full understanding of why the buyer appreciates getting the information needed to issue a letter of credit.

**"This profitable deal is too good
for a bank
to turn down the financing."**

See Story #26

Story #26

Back to Back Letters of Credit

Learning Objective:
- a) To have an understanding of a variation of letters of credit
- b) Key Terms: Collateral, Back to Back Letters of Credit

Many a banker has experienced a scenario similar to the following: A company, usually a middleman operation, claims to have made a big export sale. Since they are undercapitalized, they do not have the finances to purchase the product so it can be resold at a handsome profit. They do have, or claim they can get, a letter of credit in payment of the sale once the goods are shipped.

They approach a bank thinking this profitable deal is too good for a bank to turn down the financing. First, they request a bank to make an advance, or a loan, since the source of repayment will be a letter of credit. They soon learn, however, that banks in the United States do not make loans against letters of credit. Why? Because of performance risk. What if the exporter fails to perform precisely according to the terms of a letter of credit? They risk not getting paid and the bank will not be repaid for its loan.

Not easily deterred however, the exporter comes up with the next best idea. Since they have a letter of credit in hand, they request the bank to issue a second letter of credit to the supplier of the product. The first letter of credit would be the collateral for the second letter of credit. This gives it its name, "back-to-back" letters of credit. Sometimes they are called primary and secondary letters of credit or mother and baby or master and secondary letters of credit. Since a U.S. bank will be reluctant to make a loan against a letter of credit, it will also be reluctant to issue a back to back letter of credit. Again, what if the bank is in a position of having to pay on the secondary letter of credit but is unable to collect on the primary letter of credit? Over the years, there have been enough "war stories" to scare off most bankers.

Very few, if any, U.S. banks will entertain the notion of issuing back to back letters of credit. This practice may vary in different countries and is, in fact, quite routine in some Asian countries. In my experience, any bank in the U.S. that is willing to do so, issues back to back letters of credit only for well established customers who have proven their ability and expertise to perform correctly.

> **"We disregarded the phrase until something about it caught our eye."**
>
> See Story #27

Story #27

Was the Whole Family Stow-aways?

Learning Objective:
- a) To have an understanding of the cornerstone of strict compliance
- b) To understand Article 32 of the UCP
- c) Key Terms: Letter of Credit, "Clean" Bill of Lading, Transport Document, UCP, Ocean Bill of Lading

Often a letter of credit contains some technical wording that doesn't seem to mean very much except to the bank's letter of credit specialist. One of the technical requirements is that a transport document be "clean." What is a clean bill of lading? As usual, we go to the UCP for an answer.

Article 32a states: "A clean transport document is one which bears no clause or notation which expressly declares a defective condition of the goods and/or the packaging." In other words, an unclean bill of lading would be one which has a notation such as, "Carton number 8 is broken," etc. When the transport company accepts goods, they do not inspect the contents, but they do visually inspect the outside of the packaging. If there is damage when they receive it, the transport company does not want to be held liable for the condition of the merchandise. Hence, the notation. When a letter of credit calls for a clean bill of lading, the bank will simply examine the bill of lading for any such notations.

Some shippers, or their freight forwarders, do not understand the definition as given in the UCP. We have seen bills of lading marked with the word "clean," which of course, means nothing. The bank looks for notations which expressly declares a defective condition, not for the word, "clean."

One shipment in particular got our attention. It was a shipment of diapers from Brazil to the United States. Our bank issued a letter of credit for the payment which required a "Clean On Board" ocean bill of lading. The shipping company was careful to place the word "clean" in a conspicuous place. Of course, we disregarded the phrase until something about it caught our eye. It was misspelled, and the notation read "Clan on board." It made us wonder if, along with diapers, the baby, or even the whole family was on board. Perhaps, as stow-aways!

> **"A confirmation is only valuable
> if a second bank
> in a second country
> adds their confirmation."**
>
> See Story #28

Story #28

When a Confirmed Letter of Credit Isn't

Learning Objective:
    a)   To understand sovereign and commercial risk
    b)   Key Terms: Confirmed Letter of Credit, Sovereign Risk, Commercial Risk, Issuing Bank

Previous stories have discussed the why's and how's of having a letter of credit confirmed. Banks who confirm letters of credit do charge fees which are often an expense paid by the beneficiary. How much protection is a beneficiary receiving for the payment of that fee?

The confirmation fee is similar to an insurance premium. It provides protection against non-payment due to default because of sovereign risk or commercial risk. In other words, it protects against the issuing bank going bankrupt or the foreign government intervening in some way to prevent payment from being made. Therefore, a confirmation is only valuable if a second bank in a second country adds their confirmation.

Many exporters ask for confirmed letters of credit when they receive letters of credit issued by banks in foreign countries. Occasionally, they receive a letter of credit issued by the foreign bank that sends it to their branch in the United States for confirmation. When the exporter receives the letter of credit it does have a cover letter from the branch stating the letter of credit has been confirmed. How valuable is this confirmation?

The confirmation is not made by a second bank. The fact that it is in a second country seems immaterial. Will the branch stand behind the letter of credit in the event of default by their government or by the parent bank? Will they even be around to fulfill their obligation? It seems unlikely. In my opinion, the beneficiary has paid a fee with no protection in return.

> **"The price quotes he had were a mixture of Incoterms."**
>
> See Story #29

Story #29

Mismatched Gardening Gloves

Learning Objective:
- a) To learn the importance of the beneficiary being proactive in establishing a letter of credit
- b) Key Terms: Letter of Credit, Application, Beneficiary, Free On Board (FOB), Cost, Insurance and Freight (CIF), Incoterms, Amendment, Proforma Invoice

A gentleman appeared in the international department and identified himself as Richard, an existing bank customer, who was a distributor of goods sold in retail hardware stores. A short while ago, he said, he purchased samples from a factory in Korea and now wanted to place a large order. The factory informed him they would ship the goods upon receipt of a letter of credit. He was directed to my office.

I took out a blank application for a letter of credit and told him I would help him complete the application since it was his first one. So we started at the top. I asked for the name of the beneficiary. "Beneficiary?" he asked, "What is that?" I explained that was the party who was to receive the letter of credit, in this case, the factory in Korea. He searched in his briefcase and we found their name on the invoice for one of the shipments of the sample products.

Then I asked him for the amount of the letter of credit. "Well," he said, "we are going to have to figure that out." He reached into his shirt pocket and found a piece of used adding machine tape which he had retrieved from a wastebasket in his office. He had entered his warehouse and taken inventory on the backside of the tape. He started with the first item on the list, "I have three rolls of wire in inventory." "Okay," I asked, "How many should you have?" "Fifty." "So you need to order 47, right?" I asked. "That's right," he said. "How much are they?" I asked. "Well," he said, "we are going to have to figure that out." He found a price on an old invoice and we calculated the extension.

"What else do you need?" I asked. We continued the same procedure with each item. After several items, I noticed Richard was using some prices with FOB quotes and others with CIF quotes. I informed him that by using different Incoterms we were mixing apples and oranges and suggested we try to be consistent. Unfortunately, the price quotes he had were a mixture of Incoterms. It was the best we had. I assured him we could expect the letter of credit would need to be amended.

When we completed the extensions, I added the totals and said, "Richard, it looks like the amount of the letter of credit will be $37,846.53." "Yep," he said, "that's exactly what I thought it would be!"

On another occasion, he wanted to open a letter of credit for the purchase of some gardening gloves. From his briefcase he retrieved six sample gloves. He set them out in a row on my desk. They were basically identical except for the colors of the markings. "Roy," he said, "I want to order two styles. Which two do you think I should order?"

I answered, "Richard, I can't do that. If I choose two and they don't sell, who are you going to blame?" "Oh, I wouldn't do that!" he said. "Well, I am not going to decide," I told him. "Okay," he said, "then just tell me which two you like!" I said, "I guess I can do that." Since they all looked alike to me, I simply chose two at random and he ordered those two. To express his appreciation, he gave them to me as a gift. I used them in my garden for a number of years. Fortunately one was for the right hand and one for the left, although, of course, the coloring did not match.

After several such encounters, my manager said to me, "Roy, you are giving too much time to Richard. Why don't you give him a supply of blank applications so he can complete them before he comes in to the bank." Richard seemed grateful for the forms, and he did bring his own application along with him on his next trip, blank as can be. I guess he felt he was paying us a fee and he wanted to get his money's worth.

Our objective stated at the beginning of this story is to emphasize the importance of being proactive in a letter of credit transaction. Do you think Richard might have had a much easier task if the seller had provided quotes with some guidelines for the letter of credit? As it was, the seller left it up to the whims of Richard and me. A scary thought indeed. Exporters, please note the benefit of being proactive. Provide your buyers with proforma invoices, which include instructions on how to issue letters of credit. Their appreciation will be unending.

Story #30

How I Learned Never to Make Sales Calls With Chinese Food on my Tie!

Learning Objective:
   a)   To appreciate humor in the workplace

In today's high-stress workplace, one of the best antidotes for stress is humor. We need to see the humor in everyday happenings around us. We need to take our work seriously, but not ourselves. After all, we are biodegradable.

A friend of mine, Terry, introduced me to a Chinese restaurant in downtown Denver. He also suggested I try a menu specialty, the Mongolian Barbecue. As we enjoyed our lunch, I noticed that I had spilled some food on my tie. With a paper napkin I tried to wipe it off. Of course, the stain grew bigger and deeper. I said to Terry, "Now look what I've done." He said, "Don't worry, Roy, it doesn't show very much." I replied, "But Terry, I have to make a sales call with a commercial banker right after lunch!" Then I tried the old "do your laundry in the restaurant" trick and dipped my napkin in my glass of water and tried to wash my tie with it. Of course, the stain got bigger and it got deeper. Terry tried again to console me, "Really, Roy, it doesn't look that bad, no one will even notice."

"Terry," I said, "this is not an ordinary sales call. We have an appointment to meet with the president of a company. He designs, makes, and sells neckties!" Terry was quick to respond, "You need a new tie!" However, I didn't have enough money with me to buy one, and I had only minutes left before I would meet the lender so we could go to the company together. Then Terry came to the rescue. "There is a store at the other end of the mall. All items sell for under $6.00. I was in there just the other day and they had fake silk ties for $2.00. They really looked pretty good. If you leave right now you'll have enough time to go to the store and make it back to the bank in time for your appointment." I had $2.00 on me and it seemed like the right solution. I hopped on a Mall shuttle bus, hurried into the store, found a tie, returned on a shuttle bus, arrived at the bank, went in the washroom and changed ties. I was back in my office just as the commercial lender stopped by to ask if I was ready to go.

We arrived at the company, introduced ourselves to the receptionist who ushered us into the conference room and asked us to wait for the president. The conference room was ornate with cherry-wood furnishings. The wait seemed interminable – he kept us waiting 30 minutes, or more. Finally, a side door opened to the conference room and in walked the president. He was dressed in his finest and walked with an air of superiority.

The president began by telling us about his normal workday. He told us he arrives at 9:00 a.m., proceeds directly to his office, closes the door, pours a glass of wine, works on new designs for ties, and takes no calls or appointments until noon. He sends the new designs to England where the fabric is made. The material is then sent back to the company for cutting and sewing.

He went on to tell us that he only allowed retail stores to carry his ties if they agreed that he could do a half-day training for the salespeople on how to sell ties. I thought to myself, "A half-day training on selling ties? What do you need to know?" He must have read the look on my face because he went on to explain, "The reason I insist on the training is because my ties sell for $45 and up. They will be displayed beside some cheap $15 ties. The salespeople need to be able to persuade the customer on why he should buy one of my $45 ties rather than a cheap $15 tie."

Now, when he said, "cheap $15 tie . . .," I wanted to cover up my tie with my hands and slide under the table. I knew, at that moment, we would not make a sale. I wasn't fooling this man. He knew I was wearing a fake silk tie that cost $2! I was right. We didn't. I learned an important lesson on wearing proper attire when meeting a client.

Story #31

Khaki Pants that Will Keep You in Stitches

Learning Objective:
    a)   To understand the cornerstone of strict compliance
    b)   To learn that the applicant is not a party to the letter of credit
    c)   Key Words: Letter of Credit, Application for Letter of Credit, Beneficiary, Discrepancies, UCP

A company, which is in the garment business, found a new source of supply from a factory in South Korea. The factory informed the company that they would ship the goods as soon as they received a letter of credit. A bank for which I worked, issued the letter of credit based on the instructions the customer gave us in the application for the letter of credit. This also happened to be his first letter of credit transaction.

About two weeks later he called and asked to speak to me. He said, "Roy, I don't want you to pay on the letter of credit." I told him that since we had not yet received documents from the factory, we had not made any payments. I informed him, however, that if we received documents that met the conditions of the letter of credit, we would be obligated to pay. His sigh indicated this was not an acceptable answer, so I asked, "What is the problem with the letter of credit?"

He explained, "I received a shipment of samples from the early production line. The pants have a large pocket sewn to the outside of each pant-leg. Then sewn to the large pocket is a smaller pocket. However, the stitching from the smaller pocket goes all the way through to the pant-leg, making the large pocket useless. If I accept the shipment, I will have labor costs to remove and re-do the stitching. It will eat up all my profit and more. I can't afford to let you pay on the letter of credit."

I responded, "I understand your dilemma. However, I need to explain something about letters of credit to you. When a bank issues a letter of credit, we are saying to the beneficiary, 'If you present documents as required in this letter of credit, we will pay you.' It is as simple and straightforward as that. I can only refuse documents if the beneficiary presents documents with discrepancies. Now that I've said that, I will also tell you that in my experience, at least 50 percent of the time, we can find discrepancies. The discrepancies we may find will have nothing to do with the stitching, but we can refuse for those discrepancies." Although, my in-house legal counsel probably would have disapproved of that conversation, or my next action, I took a red marker and made a big notation on the outside of the file folder, "FIND A DISCREPANCY" and returned the file to the filing cabinet. I'm not sure my customer was at ease with this answer but the next step was simply to wait for documents to arrive at the bank.

Three weeks later one of my co-workers appeared at my desk. She had the folder in her hand along with documents, and asked, "Roy, is this your hand-writing on the folder?" I answered, "Yes." "Well," she said, "I just checked the documents and found eight discrepancies." I smiled and said, "He is really going to be happy. Let me call him."

I called the customer and said, "You can sleep well tonight. We found eight discrepancies. We'll refuse payment and return the documents to the Korean bank." Then, to my surprise, he said, "Oh no, no, don't do that! I changed my mind! I want the goods after all." That was fine with me. I didn't care why he wanted the goods, so I didn't ask. Perhaps the factory caught the error before they ran full production. Perhaps they offered a discount on a future order.

The reason I didn't care is because a bank deals in documents, not in goods. If the documents comply, we pay. If they don't, we can refuse payment or obtain the buyer's waiver. In this case, by waiving the discrepancy, he authorized payment and was able to take possession of the goods. The procedure of handling discrepancies and acceptance or refusal of the documents is addressed in UCP article 14.

This story debunks a common notion that there are four parties to a letter of credit: the applicant, the beneficiary, the issuing bank, and the confirming bank, if any. The applicant is not a party to the letter of credit. Initially, this may appear illogical. However, if the applicant was a party to the letter of credit, my customer could have stopped me from paying, even if the documents were in perfect order. Would such a letter of credit be acceptable to the beneficiary? If so, it sounds more like a revocable letter of credit to me. Although not explicitly stated, the UCP supports this concept with article 9.d.i., which states, "Except as otherwise provided by Article 48, an irrevocable Credit can neither be amended nor cancelled without the agreement of the Issuing Bank, the Confirming Bank, if any, and the Beneficiary." Note: the applicant does not have to agree to an amendment.

Story #32

How I Won a Telemarketing Award

Learning Objective:
  a)   To appreciate humor in the workplace

I have always appreciated co-workers who have a sense in humor and display it whenever they can, either through witty comments or practical jokes on co-workers. I try, as best I can, to be a good sport when I am the brunt of a practical joke.

A few years ago, I was given the responsibility to develop a brochure for our department. Since the marketing department did not understand our services or buzzwords, they relied upon me to develop the content while they developed the style and layout. I took the responsibility seriously and checked and re-checked the data on the draft of the brochure.

Finally it went to print. The printing company printed the information on a beautiful brochure. It was stiff paper and had a nice blue glossy shine. A box containing several hundred brochures was delivered to my office. I took a handful, walked out of my office, into the letter of credit department, and handed one to each employee for their future use and instructed them, "Be sure to include this brochure with mailings to customers." Then I returned to my office.

My office was configured in such a way that as I was working at my credenza, my back was to the door. I became aware of a slight commotion outside my office and turned to find several employees standing outside my door. I asked, "What do you want?" "We want to know when the bank changed its telephone number," they said. I argued with them, insisting that the bank had not changed its number. "But look at this," they said as they showed me the backside of the brochure. Listed in bold print was my home telephone number! I proofread the brochure dozens of times. It looked good to me.

The final blow came at the end of the month when our department head conducted the department's monthly sales meeting. The agenda prepared ahead of time had an item entitled "Telemarketing Award." It was to be presented by the manager of the bank's marketing department. I saw her walk into the meeting with a box in her hand that looked as if it might contain a child's toy, which I figured was going to be a gag award. I relaxed because both God and I knew I hadn't done any telemarketing that month. She announced, "This month we have an award for the person who went over and above the call of duty when it comes to telemarketing. We believe that anyone who is willing to subject his wife and children to business calls at home should have a special award." Then she reached into the box, pulled out a toy telephone, and said, "Roy Becker has graciously provided the bank's international customers with his home telephone number and is deserving of the award!" Its great to have humor and, best of all, be willing to laugh at yourself.

> **"A standby letter of credit
> is paid in the event of nonperformance
> by the applicant."**
>
> See Story #33

Story #33

A Letter of Credit Used in an Organ Transplant

Learning Objective:
    a)   To learn the different types of letters of credit
    b)   Key Words: Letter of Credit, Standby Letter of Credit, Beneficiary, Commercial Letter of Credit, Documentary Letter of Credit

I received a call from the administrator of the University of Colorado Health Sciences Center. He said they had a patient from Italy on whom the CU center was to perform an organ transplant. The patient claimed she had coverage from an insurance company in Italy. He was concerned about the coverage on the policy and his ability to process a claim. We discussed the possibility that his patient may be able to have her bank in Italy issue a letter of credit to guarantee payment. In this case, I suggested a variation of a letter of credit, a standby letter of credit. After discussions with her, it was determined to be the best alternative. She requested her bank to issue a standby letter of credit in favor of the University of Colorado Health Sciences Center. As the beneficiary, CU would be able to collect payment on the letter of credit with a simple statement as follows: "We hereby certify we have performed the transplant and have been unable to collect payment from the insurance company."

The intent of a standby letter of credit is that it will never be used. Hence, the name, "Standby Letter of Credit." It is unique from a commercial (sometimes referred to as a "documentary" to distinguish it from a "standby" letter of credit) letter of credit in that respect. A commercial letter of credit is paid when the beneficiary performs (ships goods and presents documents that comply with the terms and conditions of the letter of credit). A standby letter of credit is paid in the event of nonperformance by the applicant. In this story, if the patient's insurance company would not pay, then CU would draw on the letter of credit. The insurance company apparently paid because the University made no demand against the letter of credit. This is typical. If a standby letter of credit is used, it is because there is an issue concerning nonperformance, or in this case, nonpayment.

> **"Banks are very fussy about titles of documents."**
>
> See Story #34

Story #34

What is an Engineer's Certificate?

Learning Objective:
    a)   To understand how the UCP defines documents
    b)   Key Terms: UCP, Documents, Letter of Credit

I received a call from a company who had a letter of credit in payment for a shipment to Taiwan. She said she had some questions about the documentation requirements. I retrieved the file and asked her what was her question.

She asked me to read the requirement for document number four as listed on the letter of credit. I read it aloud to her, "Engineer's Certificate." She asked, "Can you explain what is an Engineer's Certificate?"

I asked her, "Don't you know?" She replied, "No." I said, "Neither do I!"

Then I suggested that she prepare a document properly entitled, "Engineer's Certificate." I justified that because article 21 of the UCP states, "When documents other than transport documents, insurance documents and commercial invoices are called for, the Credit should stipulate by whom such documents are to be issued and their wording or data content. If the Credit does not so stipulate, banks will accept such documents as presented, provided that their data content is not inconsistent with any other stipulated document presented." Therefore, the content of the Engineer's Certificate could say anything, as long as it did not conflict with any other documents.

I explained to her that banks are very fussy about titles of documents. In this case, the document would properly be titled, "Engineer's Certificate," and the data content could say anything as long as it is not inconsistent with any other documents.

> "If a beneficiary presents documents under a letter of credit, they are implying conformance to the letter of credit."
>
> See Story #35

Story #35

The Only Thing Hotter than a Hot Potato Is a . . .

Learning Objective:
    a)   To understanding the cornerstone of strict compliance
    b)   Key Terms: Letter of Credit, Confirmed Letter of Credit, Documents, Discrepancies, Beneficiary

One of the banks I worked for received a letter of credit for $22,000 from Belgium for a shipment of potatoes from the Red River Valley, along the border of Minnesota and North Dakota. Our bank was asked to confirm the letter of credit, which we did. The letter of credit happened to be issued in the French language.

The exporter, in North Dakota, called and asked if he could fly in to our city, deliver the documents, wait while we examined documents, and receive a cashier's check before he would return on a flight later that same day. We assured him we could accommodate his request if his documents were in order.

When he arrived with the documents, we asked one of our employees, Marcia, to check the documents because she had majored in French. The beneficiary took a seat beside her desk and watched her as she checked the documents. She made note of the "discrepancies," which he aggressively challenged. Because Marcia was interpreting from the French language, she came across several situations which were a bit confusing. For example, it wasn't clear if the letter of credit required two documents, a weight certificate and an inspection certificate, or if one document which was both a weight certificate and an inspection certificate would suffice. The beneficiary had presented only one which he said was all the buyer needed to get the goods through customs in Belgium.

Marcia finally decided the documents were acceptable, paid the beneficiary with a cashier's check for $22,000, and he left for the airport. We couriered the documents to the Belgium bank and informed them we had taken the money out of their account with us and had paid the beneficiary.

We received a communication from the Belgium bank a few days later informing us they were refusing to honor the payment and requested us to reverse the entry to their account. They stated the documents were unacceptable because of discrepancies. They went on to list eight discrepancies and notified us they were holding the documents at our disposal. As we reviewed the eight discrepancies, we felt four were unfounded. The other four, however, were a judgment call and were difficult to dispute. One was the condition that they indeed wanted two documents for a weight and an inspection certificate.

Running a bit scared, we contacted our legal council for advice. His advice was to sue the beneficiary for nonperformance. We countered that since this was a confirmed letter of credit and we had (perhaps wrongly) examined documents and found them in order, did we really have the right to sue? He reached for one of the many volumes on his shelves and found a court case that ruled if a beneficiary presents documents under a letter of credit, they are implying conformance to the letter of credit. (Otherwise, arguably, why would they present documents?) Since the documents obviously did not conform, we could sue for wrongful presentation. Reluctantly, we instructed our lawyer to contact the beneficiary who wisely said, "You'll need to talk to my lawyer." Upon contacting his lawyer, it was learned the beneficiary was declaring bankruptcy and we would get nothing even if we sued.

We contacted the issuing bank and asked them to arrange storage of the goods while we determined a solution to this dilemma. We received a message from them stating they were unable to comply with our request. When the shipment of potatoes arrived in port, the government inspected them, found they were rotten and ordered destruction of the goods. Apparently the potatoes had frozen while enroute through the Great Lakes. The bank reminded us again they were still holding the documents which gave us title to the goods, but which were now non-existent!

It was now obvious why payment was refused on some insignificant discrepancies found in the documents. Obviously, the buyer received notice of the rotten potatoes, went to the bank and instructed them to find something wrong to refuse payment since they did not want to have to pay for rotten potatoes.

We tried one other avenue. Since the goods were insured, we contacted the insurance company and notified them we were filing a claim for rotten potatoes. The insurance company was quick to respond that the insurance coverage did not include the freezing of potatoes. Since we had no other options we took the $22,000 loss.

This story complements story numbers 14 and 31. It simply looks at the cornerstone of strict compliance from another party's perspective.

Story #36

They Thought They Were Importing Cue Sticks, What They Got Was . . .

Learning Objective:
    a)   To understand a letter of credit is payable against presentation of documents only
    b)   Key Terms: Letter of Credit, Documents, Discrepancies

This story was related to me by a Chicago banker and is a classic illustration of an important principle of letters of credit. A company imported cue sticks from a factory in Taiwan. Payments were made on a letter of credit. Every presentation of documents had discrepancies that required the bank to obtain the importer's "waiver" of the discrepancies before the payment could be made (see UCP article 14). The buyer sensed an opportunity and took one or two days before giving permission to the bank. In the meantime they contacted the seller in Taiwan and requested a discount on a future shipment before they approved the payment in hand.

After some time, the factory in Taiwan apparently had their fill of these antics. On a subsequent shipment they prepared a set of documents which complied perfectly with the terms of the letter of credit. With no discrepancies, the bank did not have to obtain the buyer's approval, so they made payment and released the documents to the buyer. After bringing the goods into their warehouse, the buyer discovered the cartons did not contain cue sticks, but instead were filled with tree branches!

While the seller probably got fair revenge, it is not likely the two companies did any future business with each other, and I do not endorse the actions of either party.

This story illustrates that the bank is not responsible for the goods but deals in documents only (see UCP article 4). The bank doesn't care where the goods are or even if they exist at all. Discrepancies in the documents provide an opportunity for the buyer to refuse payment even though the goods are in order. Clean documents, on the other hand, require a bank to make payment even if the goods are defective in some way. The buyer does not have recourse to the bank if the documents are clean but the goods are defective. Their only recourse is against the seller, including possible litigation.

> **"This story illustrates the autonomy of a letter of credit."**
>
> See Story #37

Story #37

How a Transposition Cost $300,000.00

Learning Objective:
    a)   To understand that a letter of credit is autonomous from any underlying contract
    b)   To learn the varied uses of letters of credit
    c)   Key Terms: Bid Bond, Standby Letter of Credit, Performance Bond

The following story is another I first heard from Jim Harrington. A government buyer in Korea, Office of Supply of the Republic of Korea ("OSROK"), let out bids for the purchase of soybeans. Each bidder was required to post a "bid bond" equal to one percent of its bid. A U.S. company decided to enter a bid totaling $30,000,000 which required a bid bond of $300,000. The company sent their bid by telegram and asked their bank to issue a "standby" letter of credit for $300,000 in lieu of the bid bond. They were notified that their bid was accepted and they were asked to fly to Korea to sign the contract. Upon inspecting the contract they found that the price of the commodity was stated incorrectly on the telegram. It stated the unit price $0.89. It in fact should have been $0.98. It seems the telegraph company transposed the numbers in the telegram. The company informed the Korean buyer they were unable to sign the contract with these terms.

OSROK, in turn, informed the U.S. company that they had already rejected all other bids. (Of course, they did. The other bids were 9 cents higher!) If the U.S. company refused to sign the contract, OSROK would draw on the $300,000 bid bond because it would cost them that much, and more, to start the bidding process all over again.

The U.S. company faulted the telegraph company and informed them they would be responsible for the payment of $300,000 whereupon the telegraph company calmly produced the agreement and pointed out that the fine print limited their liability to $500.00! As the story unfolded, everyone recognized this was an unintentional oversight and the three parties, OSROK, the telegraph company and the U.S. exporter each decided to contribute $100,000 to resolve the dilemma.

This story illustrates the autonomy of a letter of credit (see UCP article 3). OSROK had every right to draw on the letter of credit. If they had presented a demand for $300,000, the bank would have been obligated to honor it. This story also illustrates how a standby letter of credit can be used in lieu of a bid bond. It can also be used in place of a performance bond. Standby letters of credit are understood around the world and are usually acceptable in cases such as this.

See stories 33, 44, and 46 for other uses and explanations of standby letters of credit.

> "The best humor
> is when we can laugh at ourselves
> and ask others
> to laugh along with us."
>
> See Story #38

Story #38

Why Josie Heath Lost an Election

Learning Objective:
    a)   To appreciate humor in the workplace

I think the best humor is when we can laugh at ourselves and ask others to laugh along with us. Such was the case with a young co-worker of mine.

Aida moved at the age of 19 as an immigrant from the Philippines to join family members already in Colorado. One by one the extended family immigrated and moved into a house that was no longer large enough to hold them all. Aida's mother began a house search with the help of a realtor.

One day when Aida arrived home from work, she walked into the house as her mother was on the telephone with the realtor. Aida interrupted her mother to tell her that as she was riding home on the bus she passed through a beautiful neighborhood that had three homes for sale. According to Aida's observation, the same realtor had listed all three homes. When the realtor on the other end of the phone asked for the name of the listing realtor, Aida replied, "Josie Heath." The realtor was able to keep his composure as he patiently explained that those signs were campaign signs for Josie Heath who was running for a political office! This misunderstanding may have resulted in the loss of the election for the candidate.

Later, when Aida left our department, we contacted the political candidate who graciously provided a sign for us to give to Adia, complete with the autographs from everyone on our staff. I have always admired Adia'a willingness to share this self-deprecating humor with her co-workers.

> **"Exporters naturally gravitate
> to the Incoterms 'Ex Works'
> because they think it is the easiest for them."**
>
> See Story #39

> **Story #39**
>
> **The American Flag, Mother, Apple Pie, and ... Ex Works?**

Learning Objective:
    a)   To understand the importance of using the right Incoterm
    b)   Key Terms: Incoterms, RAFTAD, UCC, Ex Works, On-board Ocean Bill of Lading, Letter of Credit, Freight Forwarder, Straight Bill of Lading, Free On Board

It has been my experience that many U.S. importers, exporters AND bankers do not understand Incoterms. They do not understand the definitions or the risks and responsibilities of their favorite Incoterms which they have always loved to use. They have even less of an understanding of how Incoterms relate to payment terms. One banker told me that his bank does not try to educate their customers on the correct use of Incoterms, because "no one uses them anyway"! What is wrong with this picture? By educating customers how to use Incoterms correctly, a bank can keep customers out of serious trouble and make its own life easier as well.

The incorrect use of Incoterms is a result of misunderstanding the several sets of shipping terms existing in the United States. We have the "Revised American Foreign Trade Definitions" ("RAFTAD") which has been around since 1941. We also have trade terms defined in the Uniform Commercial Code ("UCC"). Both are valid and can be used for domestic trade. These rules have no effect outside the country, and to the best of my knowledge, have never been translated into another language. Then, for international use, we have a third set of terms, "Incoterms", (INternational COmmercial TERMS).

Let me use several anecdotes which illustrate the misuse and misunderstanding when Incoterms are used without properly thinking through the ramifications.

Exporters naturally gravitate to the Incoterms "Ex Works" because they think it is the easiest for them. After all, what is easier than saying to the buyer, "The goods are at my back door, come and get them?" One such company in Colorado received a large order from an overseas buyer. Since they were eager to accept this large order, they offered a steep discount on the Ex Works price quote to which the buyer quickly agreed. Soon however, the exporter found these goods were selling at discounted prices in a chain of U.S. retail stores. Unknown to the naïve exporter, the Ex Works term does not require that the goods be exported at all, and diversion is a real risk. It was an expensive lesson when they contacted the retail stores to arrange to buy back the goods to avoid having to compete against their own underpriced products.

Another exporter received a letter of credit with the anticipated price quote, Ex Works. However, the letter of credit was payable against an on-board ocean bill of lading from Oakland, California. Think about the risks. What if the buyer never picks up the goods? What if the goods are damaged, lost, or stolen enroute to Oakland? The exporter would never be able to collect on the letter of credit even though they fulfilled their responsibilities under the Ex Works quote.

I received a call from the credit manager of the above-mentioned exporter who asked if I would be available to conduct an in-house training seminar on letters of credit. After agreeing, I inquired, "Why do you need the training? Do you have a new staff?" He replied, "No, we want to avoid repeating a recent problem." When I asked what was the problem, he explained, "We made a shipment to Korea. We can't collect on the letter of credit because the freight forwarder won't give us the bill of lading. In fact, we have reason to believe the freight forwarder sent the bill of lading directly to the buyer and the buyer has the goods." I asked, "What was your Incoterm?" Not surprisingly, he said, "Our what?" I answered, "Your term of sale, was it Ex Works?" "Yes," he stated, "as a matter of fact it was." I replied, "Sir, you don't need training on letters of credit, you need training on Incoterms." I went on to explain that with the Ex Works quote, the buyer contracts the freight forwarder to pickup and ship the goods. The freight forwarder would only follow instructions from the buyer. In this case, the freight forwarder simply complied with the buyer's instructions to send the bills of lading directly to Korea, and the buyer took possession of the goods without paying for them. Would you be surprised to learn this transaction happened during the height of the Asian economic crisis?

Another exporter came into our bank with documents in hand expecting to collect payment immediately on their letter of credit. After a quick check of the documents we discovered they needed an on-board ocean bill of lading indicating shipment from an East Coast port. They presented, instead, a straight bill of lading issued by a trucking company showing shipment from Denver. Yes, they correctly fulfilled their responsibility defined by Ex Works, but were alarmed to find they were at the mercy of the buyer's freight forwarder to collect payment on the letter of credit. What if the freight forwarder does not provide the ocean bill of lading before the credit expires?

Another misused term is FOB. Americans have a great love affair with FOB. Our own UCC permits the use of "FOB here, there and everywhere" (author's quotes). However, Incoterms 2000 restricts the use of FOB for ocean shipments only. Remarkably, I continue to see letters of credit using the term FOB Denver, Colorado. Even with a 100-mile view from our highest mountains, I have yet to see an ocean vessel in Colorado. Of course, an exporter can present documents which comply with the letter of credit, but how will they defend their actions in case of a dispute? Certainly not by relying on the definition for FOB found in Incoterms!

Other Incoterms, as well, can cause problems if not understood. It is important that international traders and their bankers understand their responsibilities and use the correct Incoterm that dovetails correctly with the terms and conditions of letters of credit, or other agreed payments.

Frank Reynolds of International Projects, Inc., Holland, Ohio, has written an insightful book, "*Incoterms for Americans*," which I recommend in my seminars on letters of credit and Incoterms. As previously mentioned in story #13, the committee that wrote Incoterms

1990 was composed of 20 members: 19 were Europeans and one was Japanese. With a European perspective, the Incoterms read well, but not so well for Americans. His book helps to understand the terms from an American perspective and points out the pitfalls if used incorrectly. Thankfully, Mr. Reynolds accepted an invitation and has participated in the writing of *Incoterms 2000*. Information for ordering "*Incoterms 2000*" and Mr. Reynolds' book can be found in the Appendix on page 107.

> **"A letter of credit is autonomous from any other agreements."**
>
> See Story #40

Story #40

How an Oil Company Recovered Their Losses

Learning Objective:
- a) To understand that a letter of credit is autonomous from any underlying contract
- b) Key Terms: Letter of Credit, Confirmation, Autonomy, UCP

This is another story related by Jim Harrington, of (formerly) Bankers Trust Company. A major U.S. Oil Company had an operation in Venezuela. The Venezuelan subsidiary opened a letter of credit for $7 million in favor of the U.S. Oil Company for the purchase of "oil drilling equipment." As requested by the issuing bank, a New York Bank added their confirmation to the letter of credit. Before the U.S. Oil Company shipped any goods, the government of Venezuela nationalized their operation and the company was faced with a loss of $30 million.

An official from the company's finance department called the New York Bank and asked, "Is our letter of credit still valid?" The bank replied, "Of course it is. We've confirmed it." To which the official replied, "I think I have just figured out how to recover $7 million of our $30 million dollar loss." And he hung up the phone.

A few weeks later the New York Bank received documents for $7 million. The documents complied with the letter of credit and all documents correctly described the merchandise as "oil drilling equipment." The New York Bank made payment and notified the U.S. Oil Company that the money was in their account. It was then that the official admitted what had happened. He arranged for the company to find all the broken, bent and rusted equipment they could find. They shipped these goods and described the goods as "oil drilling equipment" on the documents, and received payment. Since the documents complied with the terms of the letter of credit, the issuing bank was obligated to honor the payment made by the confirming bank.

Although, I would never endorse that one should participate in a fraudulent transaction, this story illustrates how a letter of credit is autonomous from any other agreements. The UCP supports this autonomy with article 3 which states: "Credits, by their nature, are separate transactions from the sales or other contract(s) on which they may be based and banks are in no way concerned with or bound by such contract(s)…"

> **"When a buyer is unable or unwilling to pay, the exporter has four options."**
>
> See Story #41

Story #41

How Germinating Seeds Brought Ten Cents on the Dollar

Learning Objective:
- a) To understanding the risks of a documentary collection
- b) Key Terms: Documentary Collection, Sight Draft, Documents

A documentary collection works well for many transactions and provides a measure of security for both the importer and exporter. It provides security to the buyer since they do not have to pay until they have documents which provide proof the goods were shipped. It also provides security to the seller since the buyer cannot get the goods until they pay for them. Therefore, title to the goods remains with the seller. A flowchart of this transaction can be found in the Appendix on page 111. It does have risks, however, to both parties, and probably is not a good method of payment to use for certain transactions as this story illustrates.

A U.S. company made a shipment of seeds to Belgium. The documents were presented to the buyer, through banking channels, on a sight draft, which is a formal demand for payment. For whatever reason, the buyer refused to take up the documents and make payment. The goods were kept in storage while the exporter found another buyer. By the time the exporter found another buyer, moisture had seeped into the container and the seeds were germinating. The exporter hastily found another buyer and accepted 10 cents on the dollar.

When a buyer is unable or unwilling to pay, the exporter has four options: 1) renegotiate with the buyer; 2) return the goods; 3) find another buyer; or 4) dispose of the goods. Since the buyer does not have to pay (as in a letter of credit transaction), these options may not be available when the goods are of perishable nature, date sensitive, or when they are custom-made goods. In these instances this method of payment probably should not be used.

> **"Documents should contain only the information
> required by the letter of credit,
> no more, and no less."**
>
> See Story #42

Story #42

Eight Tips on How to Get Paid With a Letter of Credit

Learning Objective:
- a) To have an understanding of a basic international banking tool
- b) Key Terms: Letter of Credit, Documents, Incoterms, Application, Amendment, Freight Forwarder

Many exporters are frustrated with letters of credit because it is thought to be a "bank guarantee" of payment, only to find they have experienced delays and even non-payment. The following tips may make life easier for the exporters:

1. Provide your customer with instructions on how to issue a letter of credit in your favor, including: numbers of documents; merchandise description; partial and transshipment conditions; Incoterm; etc. See sample instructions in the Appendix on pages 109-110.

2. Request a copy of the L/C application by fax for your review before it is submitted to the issuing bank. This will reduce long delays and the expenses related to amendments.

3. Insist that the letter of credit be payable at the counters of your favorite local bank. They will be more responsive and caring than an out-of-state-bank.

4. Review the letter of credit for correctness as soon as you receive it. The review should be done by anyone involved: marketing; traffic; credit; etc. Use a checklist and a routing slip. Request amendments if the letter of credit is not acceptable.

5. Use a freight forwarder who is trained and experienced in letters of credit and who has a rapport with your bank's letter of credit staff. The freight forwarder and your bank should work as a team to serve you.

6. Foster a cooperative and friendly relationship with the letter of credit staff at your bank. Meet them personally. They will go the extra mile to please you if you are appreciative of their efforts. Don't turn them off by being pushy.

7. Documents should contain only the information required by the letter of credit, no more and no less. Excess information has the potential to cause discrepancies resulting in delays or refusal of payment. Present the documents for examination with ample time to allow for corrections, if needed.

8. Learn all you can about letters of credit. Read. Ask questions. Attend seminars. Be a scavenger to get all the information you can. Learn to avoid the pitfalls, which can delay the processing of the transaction. Read, and re-read this book.

> "A negotiable bill of lading
> is especially valuable
> if the buyer has already pre-sold the shipment
> to a third party."
>
> See Story #43

Story #43

Who Saw the Goods?

Learning Objective:
- a) To understand how a bill of lading is a title document
- b) To learn the value of a negotiable bill of lading
- c) Key Terms: Bill of Lading, Title Document, Receipt for the Goods, Contract for Delivery, Negotiable Bill of Lading, Endorsement

How do you prove you own your car? (Not that many people can, mind you, because the bank probably owns their car). You prove it with a piece of paper, the title document. It is much the same with goods being shipped. How do we know who owns the goods? With a title document, the bill of lading. The bill of lading indicates to whom the goods are consigned, the owner.

A bill of lading serves three purposes from a legal perspective. First, it is a title document. Second, it is a receipt for the goods, and third, it is a contract for delivery. Let's explore the first purpose in a little more detail.

A technique, which is often used for certain modes of shipment, is to have the bill of lading issued in negotiable form. The bill of lading will be issued to "order," instead of "consigned to." Once it is endorsed, it is negotiable and can be delivered to another party. Whoever holds the bill of lading is the owner of the goods. This is similar to the negotiability of a check. If someone writes a check to me, "Pay to the order of Roy Becker," I can cash it, or I can endorse it to someone else so they can cash it.

Although I personally did not witness the document, I heard of a bill of lading issued for a barge of soybeans shipped from St. Paul to New Orleans. There were 35 endorsements on the backside. Each party undoubtedly marked it up a dollar or two along the way. Here is the insightful question: how many of the 35 parties actually saw the goods? The answer is: two – the party that loaded the goods and the party that unloaded the goods. The other 33 did not see the goods but could they prove they owned the goods? Yes, because they had the bill of lading – the title document – in their hands.

A negotiable bill of lading is especially valuable if the buyer has already pre-sold the shipment to a third party. The third party simply "buys" the negotiable bill of lading. Since they are now in possession of the document, they can prove ownership. They are able to surrender the bill of lading in exchange for the goods, thus saving the middleman the trouble or expense of physically handling the goods.

> "We have an example of the use of an Incoterm
> which required the exporter
> to bear the responsibility of loading the goods (FOB)
> but they had no control
> over contracting the vessel."
>
> See Story #44

Story #44

Who is at Fault?

Learning Objective:
a) To understand how a standby letter of credit can be used in lieu of a bid bond or a performance bond
b) Key Terms: Bid Bond, Standby Letter of Credit, Performance Bond, Charter Party Bill of Lading, Conference Vessel, Incoterm, FOB

An exporter submitted a bid to supply 33,000 metric ton (MT) of soybeans for approximately $6.5 million to a buyer in the Middle East. As is often required in these transactions, the exporter had to post a bid bond equal to 2 percent of the bid amount, or about $130,000. Since a standby letter of credit is readily accepted in lieu of a bid bond, the exporter asked a bank, for which I worked, to issue the standby letter of credit. The bank agreed, and the exporter was subsequently awarded the contract.

The terms of the contract required the exporter to post a performance bond equal to 10 percent of the contract. Again, the bank issued a standby letter of credit, this time for $650,000. The standby letter of credit was payable against the buyer's statement that the exporter had failed to complete the transaction according to the terms of the contract.

The buyer, in turn, opened a letter of credit for $6.5 million to the exporter payable against a charter party bill of lading. A charter party bill of lading is a bill of lading issued by a shipping company that contracts to ship the goods from point A to point B. The vessel does not have a schedule of ports or dates as a conference vessel does. In most cases, the chartered vessel carries only one shipment; in this case it was a vessel completely filled with soybeans for the buyer.

The Incoterm used was FOB New Orleans. After the shipment was completed, the exporter presented the required documents and received payment of $6.5 million from the letter of credit. One month later the buyer demanded payment of $650,000 from the standby letter of credit (performance bond). They claimed the goods did not meet the specifications of the contract. It was later discovered the goods had deteriorated in quality. The exporter denied responsibility because they claimed the goods met specifications at the time they were delivered to the port, but deteriorated while in storage at the dock. The vessel was chartered by the buyer, and it was two weeks late in arriving. If the buyer had scheduled the vessel to arrive on the date agreed, the exporter argued, the goods would not have deteriorated.

Who is at fault? We have an example of the use of an Incoterm which required the exporter to bear the responsibility of loading the goods (FOB) but they had no control over contracting the vessel. Only after the intervention of a dedicated bank officer, who made a trip to the Middle East on behalf of the exporter, was the buyer agreeable to retract their demand for payment on the standby letter of credit.

> **"A lesson to be observed
> the next time the buyer
> dictates the name
> of the freight forwarder."**
>
> See Story #45

Story #45

Acme's Freight Forwarding Company

Learning Objective:
- a) Learn the risks of permitting the buyer to choose the freight forwarder
- b) Key Terms: Freight Forwarder

A company in Boulder received an order to ship goods to Chile. The buyer in Chile provided instructions that a freight forwarder in Miami would be handling the shipment from Miami to Chile. The exporter had the goods trucked to the freight forwarder in Miami and received a receipt for the goods. Later, when the goods could not be found, the exporter produced the receipt and claimed that the freight forwarder was responsible since the goods were in their possession.

The freight forwarder on the other hand, claimed that the signature on the receipt was not valid. They insisted it must have been an imposter who accepted and signed the receipt, and then disappeared with the goods.

Since the goods disappeared, the exporter never received payment. No one knows for sure what happened. However, a strong suspicion exists that the buyer and freight forwarder were in cahoots and the buyer received the goods without paying for them. A lesson to be observed the next time the buyer dictates the name of the freight forwarder.

> **"This, of course, caused a 'catch 22' for the customer."**
>
> See Story #46

Story #46

How to Create an Earthquake

Learning Objectives:
    a)   Learn that a single transaction can use more than payment term
    b)   Learn about a government program available for export financing
    c)   Key terms: Cash, Letter of Credit, Standby Letter of Credit, Collateral, Small Business Administration (SBA), Export Working Capital Program (EWCP), Guarantee

An engineering company in Boulder designs and builds "shake-tables" used to simulate vibrations and movements. Computer controlled hydraulics mounted underneath the table operate the shake-table. The computers can be programmed to simulate movements from minor vibrations to earthquakes. The tables are custom built and sold to electric utilities, equipment manufacturers, etc. The purchasers use the tables to test equipment before it is installed in their power plants and for product qualification.

The company in Boulder received an order to supply a shake-table to a ship builder in Korea. The buyer wanted the shake-table to simulate the vibrations of a ship and the motion of the waves. In this way they could test the durability of the equipment prior to installation in the ships.

Since the shake-tables are custom made to the buyers' specs, the engineering company had to invest considerable up-front money in engineering, parts, and labor. In this transaction they were able to negotiate payment terms as follows: 40 percent up front cash payment, 50 percent payable by a letter of credit upon presentation of shipping documents, and 10 percent upon acceptance of the buyer after the shake-table was installed and training provided.

The buyer in Korea had one condition for the 40 percent cash payment. They wanted a standby letter of credit for an amount equal to the down payment. The standby letter of credit would be payable to the buyer upon their certification that the shake-table had never been built. The standby letter of credit would provide assurance that the money would be returned in the event the goods were never produced and/or shipped. The supplier asked a bank to issue the standby letter of credit.

By way of a brief background, the supplier was a well established, proven, capable and well managed engineering firm. However, the de-regulation of the energy industry caused a collapse of a major market segment for this company. As a result, at the time of the Korean contract, the company's liquid collateral had weakened. This contract to Korea, was in fact, a proactive effort on their part to diversify into other markets.

When the bank received the request for issuing the standby letter of credit, it was unwilling to take the credit exposure without cash collateral. This, of course, caused a "catch 22" for the supplier. In order to get the cash payment they needed a standby letter of credit. In order to get the standby letter of credit they needed the cash. The bank partially resolved this problem by inserting wording in the letter of credit which said it would become effective upon the bank's receipt of the cash payment. However, this did not help the supplier's cash flow. If the bank was going to keep the cash to secure the standby letter of credit, the exporter would not have use of the cash and were no better off than before issuing the standby letter of credit. Enter a government program.

The Small Business Administration (SBA) of the U.S. government has a program to assist with the financing of exports. The program, "Export Working Capital Program" ("EWCP"), provides guarantees to banks to eliminate a major portion of the risk. In short, if the exporter has an order with an acceptable, firm, means of payment, and the exporter is deemed to be able to perform, the transaction may qualify for the guarantee.

Since this company had a proven track record of performance with many satisfied customers, SBA issued a guarantee, which enabled the bank to issue the standby letter of credit without the cash collateral. The company then had use of the cash for the purpose intended. SBA's guarantee also allowed the bank to advance funds over and above the standby letter of credit. This enabled the company to borrow for purchasing raw material and meeting payroll during the six months it took to build the equipment.

The shake-table, constructed on three axis, was completed on schedule, payment was received and the loan was successfully paid. Thanks to SBA.

Story #47

Eighteen Neophyte Exporters

Learning Objectives:
    a)   To understand how a transferable letter of credit can be used
    b)   Key Terms: Transferable Letter of Credit

I have been privileged to teach workshops and seminars at the World Trade Center Denver over the years. One session is for companies who are new to exporting, or exploring the possibilities. My role is to discuss the basic methods of payment used by exporters. One morning, upon completion of my presentation, a gentleman came up to me and said, "Roy, do you have lunch plans today?" When I told him I didn't, he gave me no options, "We need to have lunch."

At a nearby restaurant, he told me his story. He was considering bidding on a project in Taiwan. The Ministry of Education was planning to build the world's largest aquarium. He intended to supply the "life support systems" – pumps, valves, filters, etc. He informed me he was a sales representative, not a manufacturer. He intended to purchase the goods from 17 different vendors, arrange for the export of the goods, and manage the installation of the units in Taiwan. He wanted to know if there were any tools available to enable him to pay the manufacturers.

I asked him if he knew how transferable letters of credit worked. He didn't, so on a paper napkin in the restaurant, I drew a flowchart showing how a letter of credit issued to him could be parceled to the vendors. "This is exactly what I need to make this transaction work," he remarked.

When I asked him if he had previous experience exporting, he answered, "No." Next I inquired if any of the 17 suppliers had experience exporting, and he replied, "A few, but most of them don't." I saved my biggest question for the last, "How big will this contract be?" Only the calmness of his voice kept me from falling off my chair as he said, "About nine million dollars!"

The transaction developed successfully. He was awarded the contract and received a letter of credit in transferable form. He requested the bank to transfer it to 17 other parties. I am pleased to report that due to cooperation among all vendors, freight forwarders and banks, over 100 shipments were made and all vendors received the payments due to them.

> **"Payment terms often dictate the success of an overseas sale."**
>
> See Story #48

Story #48

Swimming Across the Pacific

Learning Objectives:
- a) To understand payment risks
- b) Key Terms: Cash, Letter of Credit, Documentary Collection, Open Account

As I found my seat on the plane in O'Hare Airport to return to Denver, I introduced myself to the passenger next to me. He introduced himself as the controller of a meat packing plant in Colorado. My international banking instincts caused me to ask, "Do you export your product?" He replied, "Yes, we export boxed beef." My next probe was, "How do you get paid." "Cash," was his short answer.

In my experience, most exporters use all or most of the various payment methods: cash, letters of credit, documentary collections and open account as dictated by market conditions. When asking the question, "How do you get paid?", I expect answers such as this: "We get paid by cash when selling to countries A and B, Letters of Credit in country C, and open account to our established distributors in countries D and E."

When my fellow passenger replied with the short answer, "cash", it caught me off-guard because I expected a more elaborate response. "Cash?" I asked. "Don't you ever ship on a letter of credit?" "No way," he said with conviction, "if I can't collect payment on a letter of credit, I'm not going to go swimming after the boat to get our goods back." A hard and fast credit policy.

One has to admire the quality of his foreign receivables. He slept well at night and never had to inform his president of a slow paying customer overseas. However, one has to wonder if this policy didn't limit their ability to expand their export markets. Certainly they had competitors who offered more lenient terms. Meeting the competition is more than pricing. Payment terms often dictate the success of an overseas sale.

> **"It is the warehouse receipt financing arrangement, which was used by "Tino" DeAngelis in the early 1960s to bilk banks and investors out of $219 million."**
>
> See Story #49

Story #49

The Great Salad Oil Swindle

Learning Objectives:
    a)   To understand bankers' acceptances as a financing tool
    b)   Key Terms: Bankers' Acceptances, Federal Reserve Bank, Readily Marketable Staples, Warehouse Receipts

One of the tools used by banks for financing international trade is Bankers' Acceptances. This financing arrangement was authorized by the Federal Reserve Bank in 1913 to allow U.S. banks to compete with London banks in the international financing arena. Bankers' Acceptances, or B/A's, have several advantages. They are short term of 180 days or less and are tied to specific self-liquidating transactions. Once the B/A has been created, a bank can sell it into the secondary market and thus maintain liquidity.

The Federal Reserve Bank specified certain transactions, which qualify for B/A financing. The transactions must relate to a shipment of goods, or secured with readily marketable staples which are stored in independent warehouses. It is the warehouse receipt financing arrangement, which was used by "Tino" DeAngelis in the early 1960s to bilk banks and investors out of $219 million.

DeAngelis was able to falsify warehouse receipts for the alleged storage of salad oil in tanks. His tanks had false or hollow bottoms with only a portion of the tank filled with oil. The swindler then used these receipts to pledge as collateral to borrow millions of dollars, which he used in an attempt to corner the cottonseed and soybean markets on the commodities exchange. Apparently, he intended to make a killing in those markets, and then use the profits to buy salad oil to legitimately fill the tanks.

DeAngelis made heavy margin purchases of soybean oil and cottonseed oil futures in the expectation that the USSR would buy vegetable oils in the U.S. However, the prices of the futures began to drop, and DeAngelis was unable to come up with the money to cover the decline in the value of the contracts. His fake warehouse receipts were examined by officials who discovered the truth. DeAngelis was charged with fraud in 1965, convicted, and given a twenty-year prison sentence. All but $1 million from the so-called "Great Salad Oil Swindle" was recovered.

> **"He who has the gold, rules."**
>
> See Story #50

Story #50

The Golden Rule

Learning Objectives:
    a)   To learn that mistakes and misunderstandings will cost money

The "Golden Rule" of international trade is very simple to understand: He who has the gold, rules. If you don't believe it, I'd suggest you read or re-read any of the following story numbers 1, 2, 8, 14, 31, 36, and 39.

> **"Exporters learn the risks of Ex Works."**
>
> See Story #51

Story #51

Why Doesn't Everyone Use DDP?

Learning Objectives:
- a) To learn methods for avoiding diversion of goods
- b) Key Terms: Incoterms, EXW, DDP

One on-going concern for many exporters is that their products may find their way into a country or market which is contrary to U.S. laws, or into the wrong hands which can be detrimental in some way. It is important for exporters to know and have trust in the party who is purchasing the goods.

At a recent workshop on Incoterms, I prepared my usual outline, using the technique of ranking the Incoterms from least responsibility for the seller to most responsibility for the seller. Initially, exporters are attracted to the term with least responsibility for them, which is Ex Works. In laymen's terms, the seller says, "The goods are at my back door, come and get them." As the workshop develops, the exporters learn that there are risks of Ex Works, one being diversion as Story number 39 illustrates.

A company in Colorado sent two employees to the workshop. They dutiful took notes but made very few, if any, comments during the course of the class, until we got to the last Incoterm, DDP (Delivered Duty Paid). Then one of them made a simple statement, "I don't understand why everyone doesn't use DDP."

The DDP term places full responsibility on the exporter and very little on the importer. The exporter must jump through all the hoops and hurdles including transportation and insurance to the buyer's facility. It is the only Incoterm that requires the seller to arrange for customs clearance on the buyer's side.

Why was this important to this company? They manufacture computer products that could be misused if the goods find their way into the wrong hands. The exporter wants to be assured that their product arrives at the intended destination and will be only used for the purpose intended. If the products are diverted into another country the exporter could be liable with some serious implications. By using DDP, the seller has complete control of the shipment to its destination and can avoid the possibility of diversion.

> **"We started with a cement story, how appropriate to end with one."**
>
> See Story #52

Story #52

The British Need Cement

Learning Objectives:
    a)   To realize not all deals are that great
    b)   Key Terms: Transferable Letters of Credit

Now we've come full circle. We started with a cement story, and now let's end with one. Over the years I have been contacted by many charlatans in the business. Greed often clouds common sense.

In my entire career, I have not seen a single successful transaction involving huge sugar or cement deals. However, the fantasy of making big money keeps these deals alive. Usually, the proposed deal involves a string of middlemen, each claiming to be in direct contact with an authentic buyer or seller. Most often, the middleman's expertise is in a non-related industry. Calls come from people involved in real estate, automobile dealers, and who knows what, and they know nothing about exporting, let alone cement or sugar. The middleman is always the person who contacts me. The buyer allegedly has offered to provide a letter of credit, which will be designated as transferable, divisible and assignable. (These words and others are often dead give-aways of a non-existent transaction.) Although, I handle these calls politely, my eyes glaze over because the story is always the same and it is apparent that the poor guy in the middle is going to lose money and time chasing these non-existent deals.

I remember a call from a gentleman in a remote mountain location in Colorado. I had previously met him and remembered him as a reasonably successful manufacturer's rep. The call began, "Roy, have you heard the British are building a tunnel to France?" Well, I listen to National Public Radio and, yes, I knew. He said the British obviously would need a lot of cement and he heard that cement was available in huge quantities in Saudi Arabia. He requested my assistance in his effort to buy the cement from Saudi Arabia and sell it to the British. After allowing him to give a lengthy discourse on his scheme, complete with how much fee income my bank would earn, I had to ask the obvious question. "If the British need cement, wouldn't they know where it is and how to buy it? Why would they need help from someone remotely located in Colorado?" To my surprise, he said he hadn't thought about that before, and yes, probably it would be futile to pursue it.

Appendix

Publications Information

"*Incoterms for Americans*", by Frank Reynolds

    Order from: International Projects, Inc.
                           P.O. Box 352650
                           Toledo, OH. 43635-2650
                           Tel. 419-865-6201
                           Fax 419-865-0954

"*Incoterms 2000*", ICC Publication No. 560
"*Guide to Incoterms 2000*", ICC Publication No. 620
"*Uniform Customs and Practice for Documentary Credits*", ICC Publication No. 500
"*International Standby Practices*", ICC Publication No. 590
"*Uniform Rules for Collections*", ICC Publication No. 522

    Order from: ICC Publishing, Inc.
                           156 Fifth Avenue, Suite 417
                           New York, N.Y. 10010
                           Tel. 212-206-1150
                           Fax 212-633-6025

SAMPLE LETTER OF CREDIT- SWIFT FORMAT

	700 Issue of a Documentary Credit
	Reference: XXXXX
To:	ADVISING BANK'S SWIFT ADDRESS
	ADVISING BANK'S NAME
From:	ISSUING BANK'S SWIFT ADDRESS
	ISSUING BANK'S NAME
27	Sequence of total
	1/1
40A	Form of Documentary Credit
	IRREVOCABLE
20	Documentary Credit Number
	XXXXX
31C	Date of Issue
	XX/XX/XX
31D	Date and place of expiry
	XX/XX/XX
50	Applicant
	APPLICANT'S NAME AND ADDRESS
59	Beneficiary
	BENEFICIARY'S NAME AND ADDRESS
32B	Currency Code, Amount
	USD XXXXX
41D	Available with...
	ANY BANK BY NEGOTIATION
42C	Drafts at...
	SIGHT
42D	Drawee
	ISSUING BANK NAME
43P	Partial Shipments
	NOT ALLOWED
43T	Transshipment
	ALLOWED
44A	Loading on Board/Dispatch/Taking in Charge at/from
	USA AIRPORT
44B	For Transportation to...
	KOREAN AIRPORT, KOREA
44C	Latest Date of Shipment
	XX/XX/XX
46A	Documents required
	1. AIR WAYBILLS CONSIGNED TO ISSUING BANK MARKED 'FREIGHT COLLECT' AND 'NOTIFY ACCOUNTEE'.
	2. SIGNED COMMERCIAL INVOICE IN QUINTUPLICATE.
	3. PACKING LIST IN TRIPLICATE
71B	Charges
	ALL BANKING CHARGES OUTSIDE KOREA ARE FOR ACCOUNT OF BENEFICIARY
49	Confirmation instruction
	WITHOUT
53A	Reimbursement Bank
	REIMBURSING BANK'S NAME
78	Instructions to Paying/Accepting/Negotiating Bank
	THE NEGOTIATING BANK IS TO CLAIM PROCEEDS FROM OUR NEW YORK BRANCH
45B	Shipment of Goods
	DISCRIPTION OF MERCHANDISE AS PER ORDER NUMBER XXXXX
47B	Additional conditions
	CONDITIONS STATED WHICH ARE RELATIVE TO THE TRANSACTION

Instructions to the Buyer for Opening a Letter Of Credit

Date: _____ Proforma Invoice: _____
Your Ref: _____ Your Ref and Date: _____

We have indicated below those terms and conditions we would find acceptable in a Letter of Credit issued by your bank. Your efforts to comply with these terms and conditions in the issuance of this Letter of Credit will assure prompt dispatch of your order. If your bank is unable to issue the credit within the following guidelines, please contact us for agreement on those areas that must be altered. This will eliminate needless costs involved in amendments and delays after the credit has been opened. Only the items marked with an "X" will apply:

___ The Letter of Credit is to be drawn in irrevocable form and is subject to the Uniform Customs and Practice for Documentary Credits, as published and updated from time to time by the International Chamber of Commerce.
___ This Letter of Credit is to be advised by:
Name of Bank
Attn: International Dept.   Telex/SWIFT information
Street Address   Telephone Number
City, State, Postal Code USA   FAX Number
___ The beneficiary is to be shown as: _____
___ The letter of credit is to be negotiable by any bank.
___ The letter of credit is to be payable:
   ___ At sight
   ___ At _____ days sight
   ___ At _____ days from bill of lading
___ The amount of the letter of credit is to be:
   ___ US Dollars_____
   ___ Other_____
   ___ Exactly
   ___ About
___ The merchandise description should read as follows:
_____

___ Transshipments: ___ Permitted   ___ Not permitted
___ Partial shipments: ___ Permitted   ___ Not permitted

Over>>

___ We agree to provide the following documents if required in the letter of credit. Any other documents must be agreed to by us prior to the issuance of the letter of credit:
___ Commercial invoice, one original and ___ copies
___ Packing list in ___ copies
___ Insurance certificate for 110% of invoice value covering all risks, war risks, SRCC, and _____
___ Other documents: _____
_____

___ Select one of the following:
   ___ Full set of clean on board ocean bills of lading consigned to order of: _____
   ___ Airway bill consigned to: _____
   ___ House airway bills allowed (air shipments only)
   ___ Multimodal bill of lading allowed
Transport document to be marked:
   ___ Freight Prepaid
   ___ Freight Collect
   ___ Notify Party: _____

___ Shipping terms in accordance with INCOTERMS 2000 (select only one):
If goods available to buyer prior to main transport:
   ___ Ex Works (EXW): _____
   ___ Free Carrier (FCA): _____
If air shipments:
   ___ Free Carrier (FCA): _____
   ___ Carriage Paid To (CPT): _____
   ___ Carriage and Insurance Paid (CIP): _____
If ocean shipments:
   ___ Free Along Side (FAS): _____
   ___ Free on board (FOB): _____
   ___ Cost and Freight (CFR): _____
   ___ Cost, Insurance and Freight (CIF): _____

___ The Letter of Credit is to specify that all banking charges:
   ___ Will be paid by the applicant
   ___ In the United States will be paid by the beneficiary

___ The documents must be presented within ___ days from the date of the transport document, but not later than _____.

___ Other special instructions: _____
_____

___ Please fax us a copy of the completed application for this letter of credit and wait for our agreement prior to delivering it to your bank.

FLOW CHART – COLLECTION SIGHT DRAFT

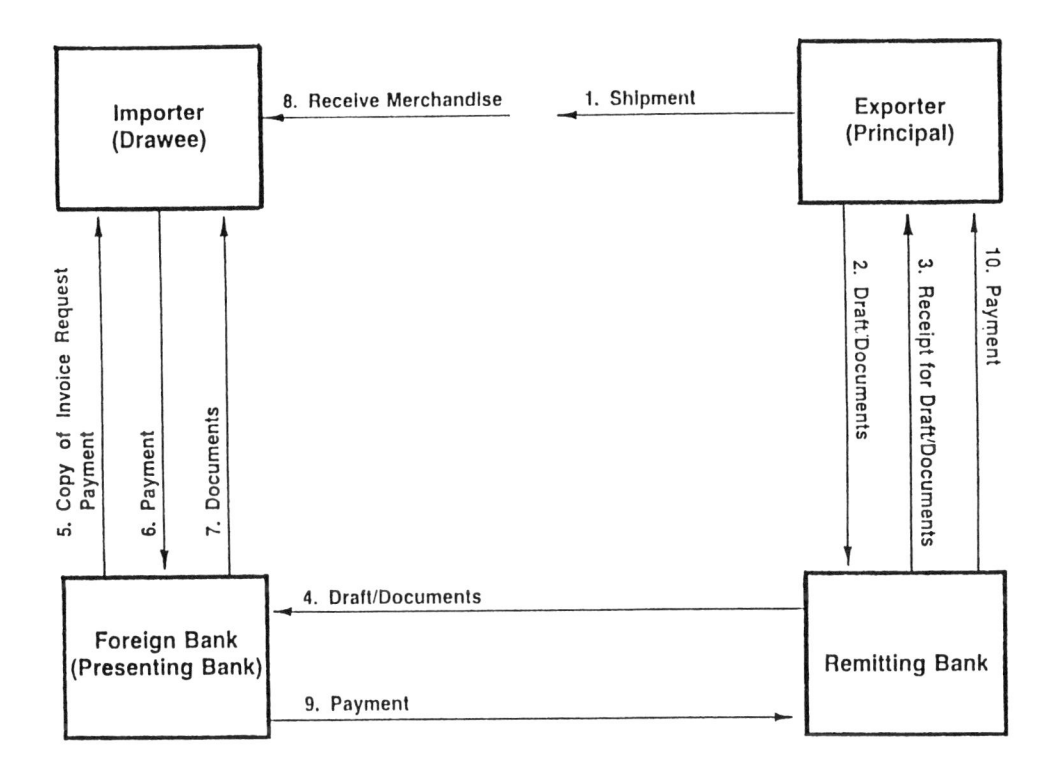

Importer (Drawee) ← 8. Receive Merchandise ← 1. Shipment ← **Exporter (Principal)**

Exporter → Remitting Bank: 2. Draft/Documents
Remitting Bank → Exporter: 3. Receipt for Draft/Documents
Remitting Bank → Exporter: 10. Payment

Importer → Foreign Bank: 5. Copy of Invoice Request Payment
Importer → Foreign Bank: 6. Payment
Foreign Bank → Importer: 7. Documents

Remitting Bank → Foreign Bank (Presenting Bank): 4. Draft/Documents
Foreign Bank (Presenting Bank) → Remitting Bank: 9. Payment

FLOW CHART – COLLECTION TIME DRAFT

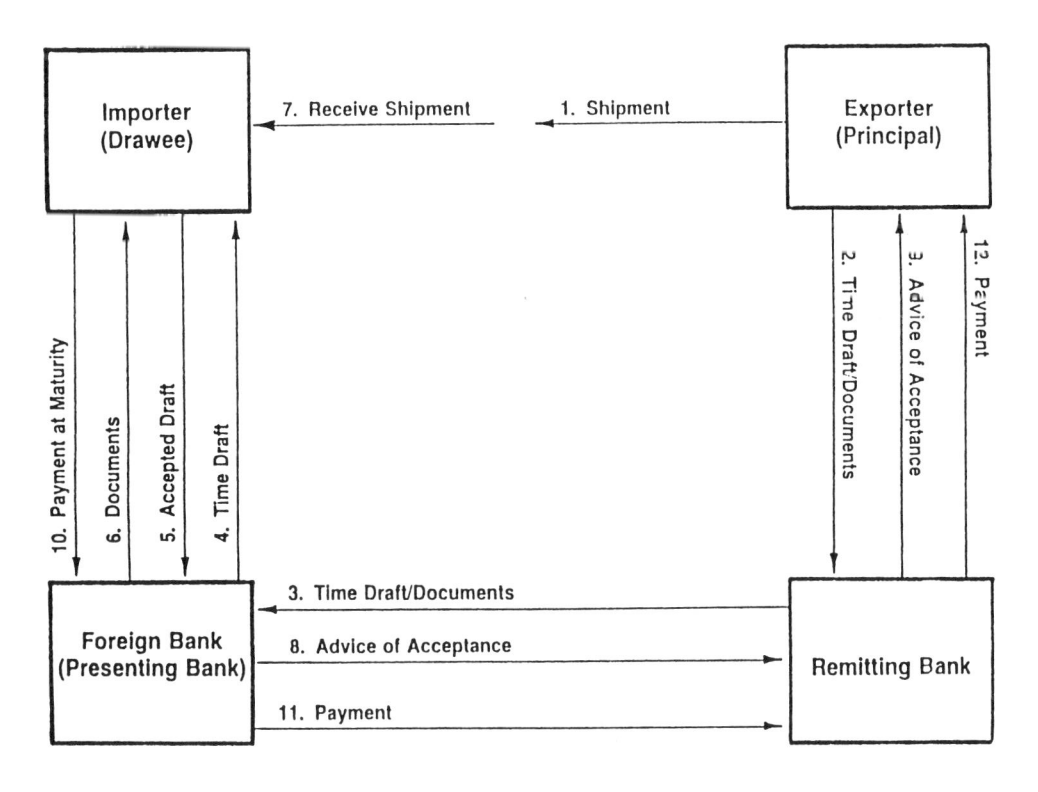

Importer (Drawee) ← 7. Receive Shipment ← 1. Shipment ← **Exporter (Principal)**

Exporter → Remitting Bank: 2. Time Draft/Documents
Remitting Bank → Exporter: 3. Advice of Acceptance
Remitting Bank → Exporter: 12. Payment

Importer → Foreign Bank: 10. Payment at Maturity
Foreign Bank → Importer: 6. Documents
Importer → Foreign Bank: 5. Accepted Draft
Foreign Bank → Importer: 4. Time Draft

Remitting Bank → Foreign Bank (Presenting Bank): 3. Time Draft/Documents
Foreign Bank (Presenting Bank) → Remitting Bank: 8. Advice of Acceptance
Foreign Bank (Presenting Bank) → Remitting Bank: 11. Payment

FLOW CHART – LETTER OF CREDIT SIGHT DRAFT

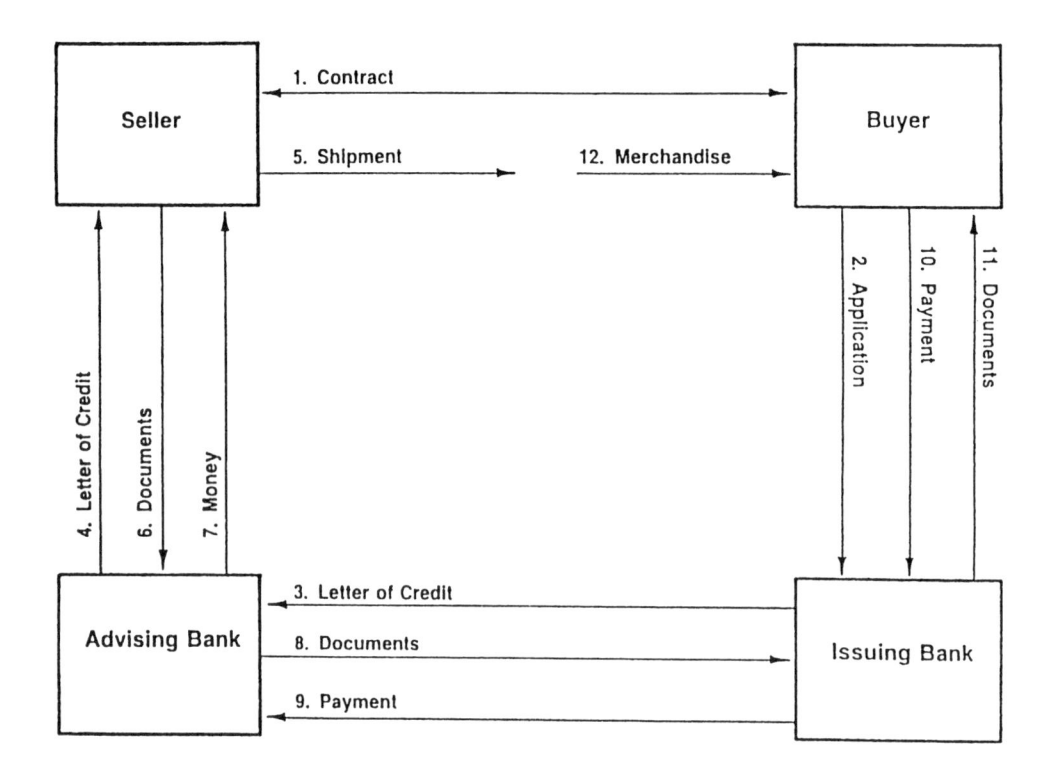

```
         1. Contract
Seller ←―――――――――――――→ Buyer
         5. Shipment      12. Merchandise
       ―――――――――→       ―――――――――→

   ↑  ↓  ↑                    ↓  ↑  ↑
   4. Letter of Credit         2. Application
   6. Documents                10. Payment
   7. Money                    11. Documents

Advising Bank               Issuing Bank
         3. Letter of Credit
       ←―――――――――――――
         8. Documents
       ―――――――――――――→
         9. Payment
       ←―――――――――――――
```

FLOW CHART – LETTER OF CREDIT TIME DRAFT

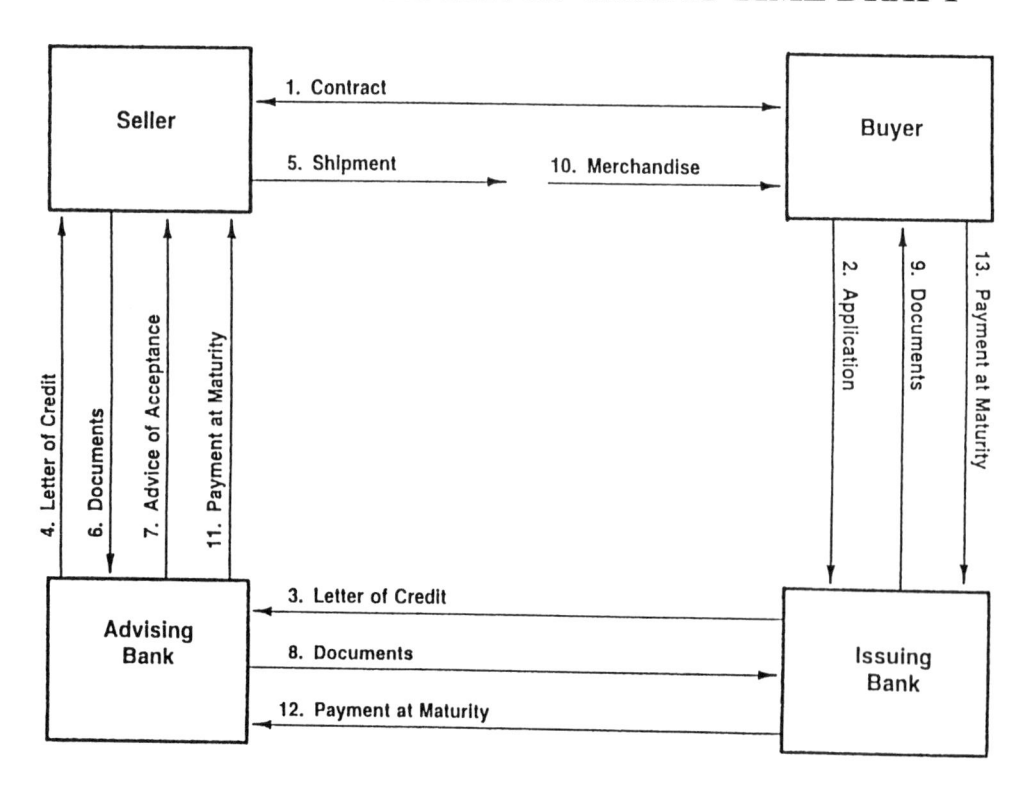

```
         1. Contract
Seller ←―――――――――――――→ Buyer
         5. Shipment      10. Merchandise
       ―――――――――→       ―――――――――→

   ↑  ↓  ↑  ↑                 ↓  ↑  ↑
   4. Letter of Credit         2. Application
   6. Documents                9. Documents
   7. Advice of Acceptance     13. Payment at Maturity
   11. Payment at Maturity

Advising Bank               Issuing Bank
         3. Letter of Credit
       ←―――――――――――――
         8. Documents
       ―――――――――――――→
         12. Payment at Maturity
       ←―――――――――――――
```

Index of Key Terms

Referenced by Story Number

-A-
Accepted Draft – 8
Advising Bank – 10
Advised Letter of Credit – 11
Air Waybill – 16
Amendment – 7, 11, 14, 29, 42
Applicant – 14
Application for Letter of Credit – 7, 25, 29, 31, 42
Approval – 5
Assignment of Proceeds – 16
Autonomy – 40

-B-
Back to Back – 26
Balance of Payments – 20
Bank
    Advising – 10
    Confirming – 1
    Intermediary – 12
    Issuing – 1, 10, 11, 28
Bankers' Acceptances – 49
Beneficiary – 3, 11, 12, 14, 29, 31, 33, 35
Bid Bond – 37, 44
Bill of Lading – 13, 17, 43
    Charter Party – 44
    Clean – 27
    Negotiable – 43
    Ocean – 27
    On board – 17
    Straight – 39

-C-
Cash (payment method) – 46, 48
Charter Party Bill of Lading – 44
Clean Bill of Lading – 27
Collateral – 26, 46
Collections – 9, 17
    Documentary – 41, 48
Commercial Invoice – 2, 14
Commercial Letter of Credit – 33
Commercial Risk – 28
Conference Vessel – 44

-C- (continued)
Confirmation – 40
Confirmed Letter of Credit – 1, 10, 11, 15, 28, 35
Confirming Bank – 1
Contract
    Sales – 2
    Delivery – 43
Consular Invoice – 24
Cost, Insurance and Freight (CIF) – 29
Customs – 5
Customs Entry – 24

-D-
DAA or D/A – 8
DDP – 51
Discrepancies – 5, 7, 14, 31, 35, 36
Documentary Collection – 8, 41, 48
Documentary Letter of Credit – 33
Documents – 2, 5, 14, 34, 35, 36, 41, 42
Documents Against Acceptance – 8
Draft, Sight – 41

-E-
Endorsement – 43
Expiration Date – 10, 24
Export Working Capital Program (EWCP) – 46
Ex Works – 13, 39, 51

-F-
Federal Reserve System (or Bank) – 9, 49
Final Clearance – 9
Free Carrier (FCA) – 13
Free On Board (FOB) – 13, 29, 39, 44
Freight Forwarder – 39, 42, 45

-G-
Guarantee – 46

-I-
Incoterms – 13, 29, 39, 42, 44, 51
    CIF – 29
    DDP – 51
    Ex Works – 13, 39, 51
    FCA – 13
    FOB – 13, 29, 39, 44

-I- (continued)
Intermediary Bank – 12
International Chamber of Commerce – 6, 13
International Wire Transfer – 12
Invoice – 18
    Commercial – 2, 14
    Consular – 24
    Proforma – 29
Irrevocable – 3, 11
Issuing Bank – 1, 10, 11, 28

-L-
Letters of Credit – 2, 5, 6, 8, 14, 16, 17, 18, 24, 27, 34, 36, 39, 48
    Advised – 11
    Application – 7, 25, 29, 31, 42
    Back to Back – 26
    Commercial – 33
    Confirmed – 1, 10, 11, 15, 28, 35, 40
    Documentary – 33
    Irrevocable – 3, 11
    Revocable – 3
    Standby – 33, 37, 44, 46
    Transferable – 47, 52

-M-
Merchandise, Description – 2, 18

-N-
Negotiable Bill of Lading – 43
Non-Sufficient Funds – 9
NSF – 9

-O-
Ocean Bill of Lading – 27, 39
On-Board Date – 17
Open Account – 48

-P-
Performance Bond – 37, 44
Presentation Period – 24
Proforma Invoice – 29

-R-
Readily Marketable Staples – 49
Receipt (for the goods) – 43
Revised American Foreign Trade Definition (RAFTAD) – 39

-R- (continued)

Revocable – 3
Risk – 1, 8, 9, 15
    Commercial – 28
    Sovereign – 1, 8, 9, 10, 21, 28

-S-

Sales Contract – 2
Sight Draft – 10, 41
Small Business Administration (SBA) – 46
Sovereign Risk – 1, 8, 9, 10, 21, 28
Standby Letter of Credit – 33, 37, 44, 46
Straight Bill of Lading – 39
Strict Compliance – 2, 14, 18
S.W.I.F.T. – 22

-T-

Tenor – 10
Title Document – 17, 43
Transferable Letter of Credit – 47, 52
Transport Document – 27

-U-

Uniform Customs and Practice for Documentary Credits (UCP) –
    2, 3, 5, 6, 11, 14, 18, 19, 24, 27, 31, 34, 40
Uniform Commercial Code (UCC) – 39

-W-

Warehouse Receipts – 49
Wire Transfer, International – 9, 12

ORDER FORM

Please send me _____ copies of *"A Banker's Insights on International Trade"*

1st copy	1	X	$39.95	= $ 39.95
Add'l copies	___	X	$34.95	= $ _____
Subtotal				= $ _____
In Colorado, add Sales Tax of 3.8%				= $ _____
Postage/Handling: $4 for first book, $2.50 each additional				= $ _____

Total $ _____

SHIP TO (please type or write clearly):

Your Name: _____
Company: _____
Street Address: _____
City: _____ State: ____ Postal Code: _____
Phone: _____ Fax: _____
e-mail: _____

Mail this form with check/money order/credit card payment for total amount to:

Roy Becker Seminars
PO Box 3042
Littleton, CO. 80161-3042
Telephone: 303-850-0625

Order by credit card: __Visa __ MC
Card Number: _____ Exp. Date: _____
Name shown on card: _____
Your signature: _____